A Practical Guide to the Balanced Scorecard

Cam Scholey, CMC, MBA, CMA

CCH CANADIAN LIMITED
90 Sheppard Avenue East, Suite 300
Toronto, ON M2N 6X1
Telephone: (416) 224-2248 Toll Free: 1-800-268-4522
Fax: (416) 224-2243 Toll Free: 1-800-461-4131
www.cch.ca

Published by CCH Canadian Limited

www.cch.ca ®

Canadian Cataloguing in Publication Data

Cam Scholey

A Practical Guide to the Balanced Scorecard

Includes index.

ISBN 1-55141-043-5

1. Organizational effectiveness — Measurement.   2. Performance — Measurement. I. Title. II. Series.

HF5657.4.S37   2002   658.4'013   C2002-900862-X
HF5657.4.S37   2002

Typeset by CCH Canadian Limited.
Printed in Canada.

Table of Contents

FOREWORD

"The balanced scorecard is like the dials in an airplane cockpit: it gives managers complex information at a glance."

Thus wrote Robert Kaplan and David Norton in their 1992 *Harvard Business Review* article that started it all, "The Balanced Scorecard — Measures That Drive Performance". Since then, scores of organizations ranging from Fortune 500 corporations to religious organizations have successfully adopted the balanced scorecard. The main objective of this book is to assist the many organizations that would like to implement a balanced scorecard solution, but have not yet done so because of the inherent complexity and difficulty in understanding how to implement one. While there is no shortage of excellent literature on the topic, one missing piece is a guide to making the balanced scorecard happen. This book is that guide.

Any human enterprise with a properly executed strategy can achieve great things. That said, how often is an organizational strategy, even a great one, actually executed down through the ranks of management and workers? Generally speaking, not very often. The balanced scorecard can be a very powerful tool in this regard.

This book is about implementing the balanced scorecard in your organization, and how you can use it to link employee's actions and compensation directly to the organizational strategy. You will provide the business strategy; this book will show you how to help people achieve it. By "cascading" the scorecard down through departments and ultimately to individuals, you can achieve a successful strategy execution. The book's approach helps you construct the organizational scorecard, then takes that scorecard and creates a separate scorecard for each department. With the new departmental scorecard, you then create individual scorecards for each employee. Think of it as an organization chart. Like the diagram below illustrates, all scorecards are created from the one directly above it. The actual number of organizational levels does not matter — the process continues until individual scorecards have been created. In this way, larger organizations can also use the solution offered in this book.

The balanced scorecard model used in this book consists of a framework and process for you to follow in implementing the balanced scorecard. Each step is integrated with the one before it. Followed properly, the probability of scorecard success increases dramatically.

An essential consideration is that a balanced scorecard means change. Not all change is embraced. Many people fear change, especially when it affects their job and compensation. So you need also to manage the change created by a scorecard implementation. This book will tell you what you can expect and guide you through it to minimize the disruption that resistance can create. Since change is also an opportunity to those people who can respond appropriately to it, the scorecard is really an opportunity for people to add more value, feel like they are making a positive difference, and be rewarded for it.

Management fads and "flavours of the month" come and go, but fundamentals stay with us forever. The fundamentals of business strategy formulation and execution remain the same. This book is about fundamentals, specifically, fundamentals regarding strategy execution. It focuses on a management tool, the balanced scorecard, and prescribes a formula to allow you to survive and prosper, regardless of the turbulence being faced under such pressures as increased competition and globalization. Once in place, the scorecard can lead to years, even decades, of success.

The future is an exciting one — the technology, the breaking down of barriers, all the new tools at our disposal. If the human potential can be unlocked to assist in achieving the chosen strategy, the future becomes even more exciting. On the other side of the coin, organizations that cannot achieve their strategy will likely yield to those that have achieved theirs. Assuming that the business strategy chosen is a good one, it's really that simple: if you achieve your strategy, you will do well, if you don't, you won't.

This balanced scorecard model grew from the realization that there was a missing piece to all the great balanced scorecard literature that exists: cascading the balanced scorecard. Regarding software, this model employs applications that most people already have on their computer. A balanced scorecard implementation is expensive and time-consuming enough — why spend any more money and training time than necessary? This book, along with the models included, provide you with the tools needed to implement a balanced scorecard solution.

Comments and questions are welcome through e-mail: cscholey@amii.ws or through the Advanced Management Initiatives, Inc. website: www.amii.ws.

Cam Scholey,
February, 2002.

Chapter 1

Introduction

Nature and Scope of Book

"In a balanced organization working towards a common objective, there is success."

— *T.L. Scrutton*

The primary objective of this book is to provide a guide that can be used to implement a balanced scorecard system of performance measurement and performance management[1]. While it is true that several excellent books exist on the topic of balanced scorecard, none provide a complete, hands-on resource for organizations that have decided to implement a scorecard system. This book does that. A fictitious company called Delphis Mobility is used throughout the book as a case study to simulate a balanced scorecard implementation. Through hands-on examples, the reader will be able to "witness" a scorecard implementation brought to life.

The balanced scorecard process can be broken down into five distinct phases:

1. Creating an organizational-level scorecard;

2. Creating department-level scorecards;

3. Creating employee-level scorecards;

4. Scoring the scorecards; and

5. Reviewing and re-creating all scorecards.

Figure 1-1 provides an illustration of the entire balanced scorecard implementation process. This book will be structured around these five phases.

☞   **Figure 1-1 provides a linear approach to scorecard implementation. In reality, it may be possible to reduce the completion time of the implementation by working on various phases concurrently. This approach is recommended only if overall completion time must be kept to an absolute minimum.**

---

[1] The term "performance management" used here does not refer to the same definition of that term used in the Human Resource (HR) area. The HR definition pertains to that area's formal monitoring of performance; the definition here expands that to include monitoring of performance by managers throughout the entire organization. That said, the balanced scorecard provides an ideal vehicle to merge the two into one sound-performance management system.

Figure 1-1: Scorecard Process Overview

Phase 1: Create the organization-level scorecard	Phase 2: Create the department-level scorecards	Phase 3: Create the individual-level scorecards

Phase 4: Score all scorecards

Phase 5: Review, re-create all scorecards

A balanced scorecard system is implemented to put the strategy into action. The main focus of the scorecard is to measure and reward employees for taking those actions that will achieve the chosen strategy. With that in mind, a major determinant of whether an organization's balanced scorecard initiative will be successful is the strategy that has been formulated. To put it another way, a balanced scorecard's results can only be as good as the strategy that it is put forth by management.

Since a good strategy is a necessary precursor to a successful scorecard implementation, it is only natural that some discussion be devoted to it. Although comprehensive coverage of strategy formulation and strategic planning is beyond the scope of this book, fortunately there is an abundance of material on this topic.[2] Chapter 2 of this book provides a short review of the essential elements of strategy that must be present in order to proceed with a scorecard implementation.

The rest of the book is dedicated to thorough coverage of the five phases of implementation discussed above. Chapter 7 covers several items the reader should consider before or while embarking upon a balanced scorecard initiative — e.g., benchmarking, which facilitates the use of external information to create target measures. The final chapter provides some ideas about how the scorecard can be merged with other popular management accounting topics, such as activity-based costing and economic earnings.

---

[2] An excellent reference is *The Strategy-Led Business* by Kerry Napuk (London: McGraw-Hill, 1993).

The Balanced Scorecard Defined

The balanced scorecard is a performance measurement and management system that is put in place to assist management with the execution of a chosen strategy. It is a performance measurement system in that it provides expectations to employees as to their role as agents of the organization, and evaluates their success or failure in this capacity. By providing "scores" based on actual results, the scorecard provides an accurate and insightful view as to how well (or poorly) the organization has performed. Of course, performance measurement is an after-the-fact analysis tool, so it is important to manage performance as well.

A performance management system is one that clearly and unmistakably provides objectives to employees, so that they in turn may use these objectives as a directive in actions taken. The balanced scorecard does this by providing specific objectives and targets to employees, thereby reducing ambiguity and mixed signals. In addition, both employees and management will be able to gauge progress toward the objectives, and be more proactive in those instances where objectives are at risk.

Scorecard Perspectives

The balanced scorecard is usually structured into specific categories, or perspectives, that represent each important area of the business and provide balance. Four commonly used perspectives are:

1. Financial,

2. Customer,

3. Internal Business Process, and

4. Innovation and Learning.

Creating a scorecard within these four perspectives, an organization will be able to attain the balance of coverage that is such an important ingredient in scorecard implementation. An organization is certainly not limited to these perspectives; many organizations have added to these by also covering domains such as the environment and the interests of internal customers.

Employee Perspective

A more recent area gaining popularity for balanced scorecard purposes is in respect to employees. While it can be said that employees are represented in many areas of the Kaplan/Norton scorecard, management can send a very strong message regarding the importance of employees by including a perspective completely dedicated to them. And while adding a fifth dimension can, in some respects, add to the complexity of the scorecard, the benefits can be well worth the effort. By formally tracking and scoring factors not otherwise attended to in any serious way, such as employee development and morale, an organization can begin to hold people more accountable for such measures[3].

---

[3] The author is currently researching and developing a set of applicable goals and measures which will be useful for adding an employee perspective to the balanced scorecard.

☞   Another way to think of the balanced scorecard is as a value chain
     created to transform "intangible assets" (skills and knowledge) into
     "tangible assets" (profits and wealth). This value chain would start
     with the Innovation and Learning perspective, go on to the Internal
     Business Process and Customer perspectives and continue on to the
     Financial perspective, also known as the "outcome" perspective.
     This approach highlights the importance of the Innovation and
     Learning perspective as a key determinant and enabler to the
     ultimate desired outcomes.

e "Balance" of the Balanced Scorecard

The balanced scorecard is usually dedicated to a "balancing act" among many opposing factors:

1. Financial and non-financial indicators;

2. Leading and lagging indicators;

3. Short- and long-term objectives; and

4. External and internal performance perspectives.

nancial and Non-Financial Indicators

Adding non-financial indicators, such as cycle time or employee satisfaction to the principles of performance makes sense, since it is these types of measures that will ultimately determine the success or failure of the organization. The balanced scorecard puts a spotlight on indicators of this nature, tying them directly to strategy execution.

The continuing relevance of financial information should be emphasized here. Financial information can continue to serve as a "check" against the strategy. In other words, if employees are doing all the right things to fulfill the chosen strategy but financial performance worsens or remains poor, management should use this information to re-evaluate the chosen strategy.

Finding the best mix of financial and non-financial indicators may not be easy and will take some time, but it is a good investment in the future of the organization to do so.

ading and Lagging Indicators

A leading indicator is information gained today that points to whether the organization will be successful in the future. Measures such as on-time delivery performance and employee satisfaction may not drastically affect financial success in the short term, but undoubtedly will have a major impact going forward. Contrast this with indicators such as profitability or return on investment, which tell only a historical tale.

All of this seems very obvious, yet time and time again it is the lagging financial information that employees and management refer to for their basic decision-making. It is only with the balance that complete, informed decisions can be made.

Short- and Long-Term Objectives

Most managers recognize the shortcomings of the "quarterly earnings mentality" by which decisions are made with the prime objective of posting the best possible quarterly results, to the detriment of future performance. Behavior such as hiring freezes, training budget cuts, and curtailed research and development takes place in an effort to "look good" to investors. This is indeed a strange practice, one that investors are generally not fooled by. As Al Ehrbar puts it, "... companies are putting themselves through needless accounting gymnastics out of the mistaken belief that investors are myopic fools who care only about the latest quarterly earnings release".[4] There needs to be a blend of long-term focus and short-term survival and prosperity. The balanced scorecard advocates this blend through a time-staggered set of objectives.

External and Internal Performance Perspectives

The financial perspective and the customer perspective are fairly public — that is, the outside world generally has a sense of how the organization is performing in these two areas. To do well in these two "external" perspectives, the organization needs to place renewed emphasis on what it is doing internally to score high externally. When it comes right down to it, organizations exist to convert internal resources, such as labour and capital, into external results. It is, therefore, only appropriate that a balance between the two be sought. By having a financial and customer perspective for each of external and internal, the balanced scorecard achieves this.

A Fifth Element of Balance: Representation

In order to be truly balanced, a balanced scorecard must satisfy a fifth maxim: that balance must be represented throughout all the areas of the organization. To achieve this form of balance, the cascading process must reach down to a level low enough that each area of the organization is represented and accounted for. Again, this seems quite logical, yet it is often the case that a scorecard implementation stops well short of representing the entire organization. Too often organizations will create one scorecard at the organizational level and impose it throughout the organization. To ensure that all areas of the organization are accounted for in (and accountable to) the scorecard process, the cascading of scorecards to the lower levels is highly recommended.

In practice the balanced scorecard is very protean in nature — there are many different approaches an organization can take in its implementation. No approach is necessarily any better than another — as long as balance exists and it is an appropriate fit for the organization, being flexible in nature should prove beneficial to the organization.

---

[4] Al Ehrbar, *EVA: Economic Value Added* (New York: John Wiley & Sons, Inc., 1998), p. 67.

igins of the Scorecard

The term "balanced scorecard" has been credited to Robert Kaplan of Harvard Business School and David Norton of Balanced Scorecard Collaborative, Inc. However, the roots of the scorecard approach can actually be traced back about a century to France, where a performance measurement tool referred to as "Tableau de Bord" originated.[5] This tool was designed as a way to make the connection between employee actions and organizational performance. More recently, the company Analog Devices started using a tool in the 1980s they called the "corporate scorecard". It was through a project with Analog Devices that Kaplan and Norton became inspired to create the "balanced scorecard". The term "balanced scorecard" has become a business shibboleth in the past decade. Many organizations claim to have a balanced scorecard because they use non-financial indicators in their performance measurement system. How many are actually truly balanced, based on the definition above, is questionable.

Another important fact is that performance measurement systems that focus on a pay-for-performance approach are also not new. They have been around for decades, and in Canada their use is actually increasing. So in terms of the basic elements of the balanced scorecard, there is very little if anything that is new — each element has been around for some time. As Anthony and Govindarajan bluntly put it, "The balanced scorecard is an example of "old wine in a new bottle." The ideas are essentially the same as performance measurement systems but are repackaged under a new label".[6] While this is perhaps an overly strong statement, the point is that Kaplan and Norton have not really invented anything new.

This is not to take recognition away from Kaplan and Norton. These scorecard pioneers do deserve credit, not just for the term balanced scorecard but also for the way they have developed a simple and understandable yet comprehensive framework. It is likely because of the appealing approach they have taken that the scorecard has taken off in the past decade. Since they introduced their version of the scorecard, it has evolved into a popular tool that many organizations have adopted, either partially or completely. They have also advanced knowledge of the linkage between strategy and performance management. In both of their books, *The Balanced Scorecard: Translating Strategy Into Action* and *The Strategy-Focused Organization*, they clearly demonstrate the importance of strategy and how a balanced scorecard system can assist greatly in reinforcing this.

c Balanced Scorecard: Benefits

Successful implementation of a balanced scorecard system can yield a wide range of results that can be realized in the near term and persist well into the future. Among the many benefits, three stand out. These are:

1. Increase in employee morale;
2. Improved customer satisfaction; and
3. Improved economic performance.

---

[5] Marc Epstein and Jean-François Manzoni, "The Balanced Scorecard and Tableau de Bord: Translating Strategy into Action", *Management Accounting*, August 1997, pp. 28–36.

[6] Robert Anthony and Vijay Govindarajan, *Management Control Systems* (New York: McGraw-Hill Irwin, 2001), p. 445.

Increase in Employee Morale

Motivation can be either intrinsic or extrinsic. Intrinsic motivation is the force from within that drives people to perform well for their own esteem and pride. In other words, people generally like to do well to feel that they have made a contribution. The balanced scorecard is an excellent tool to assist with this type of motivation. Since the scorecard is highly linked to strategy, it provides employees with the direction needed in order to understand exactly how they can contribute. People want to make a difference: the balanced scorecard provides them the opportunity to do so.

Extrinsic motivation in the business world comes largely from compensation. Employees are generally more likely to be enticed to perform better when there is pay attached to their performance. The balanced scorecard easily facilitates a pay-for-performance approach, so that employees can receive additional compensation (i.e. bonus, merit increases) by achieving high scores on their scorecards.

Morale improves when employees feel that they are motivated to perform, and are being recognized for their performance. Whether it is intrinsic or extrinsic rewards that employees seek, or some combination of both, the balanced scorecard is an excellent tool for management to provide motivation to employees.

Improved Customer Satisfaction

A major component of the balanced scorecard is the research and thought that are inherent in the construction of the customer perspective. The balanced scorecard is very useful for putting a spotlight on those actions that will assist in making customers happy. In addition, those responsible for employee satisfaction will now be held more accountable for it. This combination should lead ultimately to improved customer satisfaction.

Improved Economic Performance

It may seem paradoxical that, by taking focus off the financial results of the organization, economic performance will improve. By focusing on customer satisfaction and determining what the organization must do internally to fulfill their needs, both in the short term and long term, the organization will be able to score high on the leading indicators of success; customer satisfaction and customer retention will drive economic performance in the longer run. In addition, higher scores on lagging indicators such as market share will allow for improved economic performance in the near term. Finally, focusing on internal improvements (e.g., cycle time reduction) can yield a variety of benefits, such as reduced inventory levels and waste activity elimination, will ultimately lead to improved economic performance.

Balanced Scorecard Users

In practice, the range of organizations using the balanced scorecard is astounding. As well as the regular for-profit manufacturing companies that one would expect to adopt the tool, the scorecard has been prevalent in the banking and government industries, police forces and religious institutions. Its use in such a diverse array of industries is due to one common element among all these organizations: strategy. While each has its own unique strategy, the balanced scorecard is a tool employed to assist in implementing that strategy, regardless of what the specifics are. It is not that surprising, then, that so many have come to recognize and utilize the scorecard.

~-Profit Users — Examples

There is no shortage of balanced scorecard users in the private sector. Many banks, such as Bank of Montreal and Royal Bank of Canada, have come to embrace the scorecard as the center of their performance measurement system. Technology giant Celestica Inc. has also employed the balanced scorecard. Even The Liquor Control Board of Ontario (LCBO), a government for-profit organization, is using the scorecard with impressive results.

blic and Not-For-Profit Users

There seems to be a widespread myth that the balanced scorecard is mainly a tool for the profit-seeking, and that government and not-for-profit organizations (NPOs) cannot utilize the tool effectively. Nothing could be further from the truth. In fact, government and NPOs actually need a tool like the scorecard more than any for-profit institution. Whereas for-profit companies have financial information to give them some idea of whether they have achieved their objectives — though it may not be timely and may not tell the whole story — at least it is an indication of how they have performed. However, most government and NPOs cannot rely heavily on financial information to guide them, since they do not exist to make money. A tool like the balanced scorecard becomes ideal for these organizations, since it helps them set goals and objectives consistent with their reason for existence, and provides them with information on how well they performed based on these objectives.

Government and NPOs actually have an advantage when it comes to scorecard creation. Organizations in their industry that have adopted a scorecard system are much more likely to share the results than are profit-seeking organizations. Since these types of organizations are much less guarded about the strategy they have chosen, they seem to take pride in their scorecard and are afforded the ability to publish their results to anyone who wants to view them. This facilitates easy benchmarking and information-sharing, techniques that can be of benefit to many organizations.

blic and Not-For-Profit — Examples

While not as prevalent as in the private sector, the balanced scorecard is becoming more common in its use among public and not-for-profit organizations. The City of Winnipeg, for example, has overhauled its bureaucracy and simplified its budgeting process after using the balanced scorecard to facilitate collaboration. The City of Charlotte, North Carolina is an example of a government that has actually posted their balanced scorecard on its official website. Even religious institutions, such as The Lutheran Brotherhood, have adopted the balanced scorecard.

To summarize, there are very few organizations that cannot use a balanced scorecard approach to performance measurement and management. While some very small organizations (i.e. with 10 or fewer employees) may not find the benefits of a scorecard implementation merit the costs, most larger organizations should consider it as an approach to assist them in strategy execution.

Please see the appendix at the end of this chapter for organizational profiles on three balanced scorecard adopters:

1. The Liquor Control Board of Ontario (LCBO);

2. RBC Financial Group (Royal Bank) — Personal and Commercial Financial Services; and

3. Celestica Inc.

The Balanced Scorecard versus Management by Objectives

Many people have observed that the scorecard system is quite similar to the management by objectives (MBO) approach to performance measurement that became popular a couple of decades ago. In fact they are quite similar. Both focus on determining a set of targets, or objectives, that have been negotiated and agreed to by employees and management, and both provide rewards based on actual results as they compare to the initial objectives. This is where the similarity ends, and the scorecard becomes the superior tool. An MBO system is derived from local objectives — in other words, the objectives arrived at are determined by what seems optimal in an employee's immediate environment. They are not necessarily aligned or consistent with other employees' objectives. Contrast this with the scorecard approach, which is derived from the strategy determined at the highest level — all objectives cascaded down should be consistent with and aligned with organizational strategy. If all local objectives are aligned and consistent with organizational strategy, they will in turn be aligned with all other local objectives. Any discrepancies are due to flaws in the construction of the scorecard system, not the system itself.

Summary

This chapter has provided an introduction to the concept of the balanced scorecard. The next several chapters will focus on the implementation of the balanced scorecard. Chapter 2 will cover the first major phase of any balanced scorecard initiative: strategy formulation.

pendix — Balanced Scorecard Company Profiles

uor Control Board of Ontario: A Case Study in Scorecard Success

The Liquor Control Board of Ontario (LCBO) provides an excellent example of an organization that has done extremely well with the balanced scorecard. Competing in a retail oligopoly in the alcoholic beverage market, the LCBO reported sales of $2.7 billion in fiscal 2001 — a 44% increase from just five years ago, a result that the organization credits in part to the adoption of the balanced scorecard. The company has experienced six consecutive years of record revenues and profits.

The stated mission at the LCBO is to

... be a customer-intense, performance-driven and profitable retailer of beverage alcohol, supporting the entertaining and responsible use of our products through enthusiastic, courteous and knowledgeable staff.

The company feels that the key to success in this industry and achievement of their mission is through exceptional customer service, and that the best way to provide this is with satisfied and highly-trained employees. The balanced scorecard was introduced in 1994 as an experiment in the Finance & Administration Division, with very positive results. It was then rolled out corporate-wide in 1997 through 1998. The LCBO scorecard model initially contained three perspectives: financial, customer, and internal process. The fourth perspective, innovation, was added in 1999. The scorecard was cascaded down to the district level in the Retail division (the store network is divided into 24 districts; it was decided early on that it was not necessary for each retail store to have its own specific scorecard).

The balanced scorecard would play three main roles at the LCBO. The first was to increase employee morale. In a recent study of consumer shopping preferences, it was noted that retail employee attitude was ranked as the most important factor in determining the satisfaction of a consumer's shopping experience. Employee attitudes have improved in a number of critical areas steadily since scorecard inception. The second role of the scorecard was to improve customer satisfaction. The combination of customer-oriented programs to create a better shopping experience and an improvement in employee attitudes and training resulted in improvement in customer satisfaction.

The final key role of the scorecard was to improve revenues and profits by creating a shift in market segments from the lower-revenue segments (i.e, the "homebodics" and "price-conscious") toward the higher-revenue segments (the "home entertainers", the "outgoing and active", and the "enthusiasts"). By training employees to be product experts, it was felt that consumers might be more inclined to experiment with different products (for example, an older and more expensive wine). By educating and encouraging staff to converse more with customers, the LCBO was able to increase both revenues and profits while adhering to their mission of promoting responsible drinking.

The scorecard has been of tremendous benefit to the LCBO. In addition to the results already discussed, it has been able to significantly boost both the market size and market share. As the largest player in an oligopoly, the LCBO has been able to increase the size of the total market every year since the scorecard was introduced, has been able to increase its market share by $3/4$ of a percent to a full percent annually. Most impressive, all these results are in the wake of emerging competition from U-brews and U-vints. It is clear that the scorecard has been integral in improving the LCBO's competitive advantage position. As strategies evolve within the organization, the score-card is used to cultivate and align these strategies so that the entire organization is involved in their execution. The scorecard is given credit for strategically linking and aligning the entire organization, both across districts and from top to bottom.

Like any scorecard initiative, it has not been without some challenges. The phenomenon referred to as "measure overload" has been an ongoing dilemma. Too many measures can create a scorecard that is confusing, one where employees still don't really understand what to focus on. The choice of which measures to use can be a challenge as well. In choosing measures the key determinant must be whether the results of that measure can be influenced by employee action — if the answer is no, the measure does not really belong in the scorecard. Including a measure "just because it can be measured" it simply not reason enough for its inclusion. The LCBO continues to work on refining its list of measures, ensuring that only the best and most appropriate measures find their way to the scorecard. One of the techniques employed over the past four years is activity-based costing (ABC) to assist with the revision of measures.

Looking forward, there are some considerable plans for merging other initiatives within the framework of the balanced scorecard. In addition to the current use of ABC, the LCBO plans to employ techniques such as benchmarking and economic earnings to further enhance their scorecard system. It feels that the information gained by adding these to the system will allow them to further their competitive advantage and continue making progress with both employees and customers. The balanced scorecard allows the LCBO to define and control its own destiny.

RBC Financial Group's Personal & Commercial Financial Services: Operational Excellence

RBC Financial Group's Personal & Commercial Financial Services Business (known as RBC Royal Bank) provides a great example of an organization that has been successful with the balanced scorecard, using a framework quite different from the Kaplan and Norton model. At the end of 2000 RBC Royal Bank, RBC Financial Group's largest division, reported an average asset base of $132 billion, with revenues of $6.5 billion and net earnings of $1.2 billion. One of Canada's premier financial services institutions, RBC Royal Bank's stated objective is to grow profitable relationships in Canada and the U.S. with each customer (both business and personal) by delivering a tailored and personalized customer experience. It intends to build customer relationships and grow revenues by executing the following key strategies:

1. Accelerating customer segmentation initiatives;
2. Improving sales effectiveness;
3. Pursuing electronic offerings and relationships;
4. Aggressively managing costs by lowering purchase costs, simplifying product lines and offering customers numerous service and delivery options; and
5. Pursuing a buy/build approach in the United States.

RBC Royal Bank has witnessed increased competition due to deregulation, coupled with ever-increasing customer demands. The balanced scorecard was introduced in 1994 and would play three main roles.

First, align organizational strategies from top to bottom. All 30,000 employees of RBC Royal Bank develop personal performance plans aligned to the top-level balanced scorecard objectives. Employees' performance during the year is assessed in line with their own balanced scorecard focused plans. Employees are eligible for year-end incentives calculated using their scored performance in conjunction with total RBC Financial Group and Personal & Commercial Banking specific performance.

The second role of the scorecard process is to emphasize customer focus. The financial services industry focuses on customer satisfaction, recognizing that there are several competing financial service options a customer can easily switch to if not completely satisfied. With this in mind, RBC Royal Bank has really focused their scorecard around the customer. By focusing on the percentage of customers that gave an overall score of five out of five in regular customer surveys undertaken, RBC Royal Bank is focusing on total satisfaction of the customer as well as on what drives that performance.

The third and final key role of the scorecard is to accelerate the strategy execution process. In an industry that has become much more dynamic over the past decade, quick and deliberate execution of strategy decisions is more important than ever. The scorecard has been identified as a tool that can assist with this by communicating quick strategy rollout.

The scorecard implementation for RBC Royal Bank was less difficult than for many other organizations, since most of the information on performance and customer and employee satisfaction was already being sought, collected and used under separate processes. The challenge faced was to combine and synthesize this information into a format that would be useful in more of a balanced scorecard framework. Up to that time, the information collected had not been consolidated and was not used on both national and local levels in integrated processes. This would be the focus of the scorecard initiative.

The balanced scorecard at RBC Royal Bank consists of five strategic objectives:

1. Sales/Business Performance;
2. Management of Risk;
3. Customer Loyalty;
4. Corporate Reputation and Image; and
5. Employee Capability and; Commitment.

Each objective has identified three to five performance drivers (measures that research has shown drive the objective's performance), providing RBC Royal Bank with a complete, balanced, and well-rounded scorecard that reflects both vision and strategy. A scorecard is created at the top, and is then cascaded down through all regions, branches and business banking centers through a sales scorecard aligned to the original scorecard. As an added measure of usefulness, the scorecard system has been created so that it can be viewed and summarized either geographically or by market segment.

Like any scorecard initiative, it has not been without challenges. In the early stages, there was some skepticism about the integrity of the information going into their scorecard. Top management commitment, coupled with effective communication about the initiative and a continuous effort to strengthen information reporting, assisted greatly in the eventual buy-in from managers.

Another challenge faced by RBC Royal Bank was the risk of "measure overload" — that is, a flood of suggested scorecard measures by managers involved in the scorecard process. Too many measures create a very high risk of a scorecard that is too confusing — the meaningfulness can get lost in the detail. This too was managed closely, and the scorecard has found an optimal balance with respect to number of measures.

The scorecard has resulted in a wealth of important benefits for RBC Royal Bank. Employee morale has increased in recent years, some of the credit being given to the scorecard focus on Employee Capability and Commitment. There are three reasons for this result. First, there is the intrinsic reward for employees of understanding that they are making a contribution to strategy fulfillment. Second, the emphasis on customer satisfaction affords employees the ability to take steps to make their customers happy, which in turn creates a healthier, more enjoyable work environment for employees. And finally, the compensation system, which rewards employees for high performance, has assisted as well.

Then there are the strategic advantages of the scorecard initiative. Not only is strategy much easier to keep aligned and consistent up and down the organization, the implementation time of the latest strategies has quickened considerably, which serves to provide an advantage over the competition.

Looking ahead, RBC Royal Bank plans to exploit the emergence of powerful software solutions to continue enhancing the scorecard system even further. Plans are in place to view scorecard results on their PC, drilling down into detail at the click of a mouse. Other enhancements will come also — the scorecard at RBC Royal Bank is considered an evolutionary process. As trends change and new challenges emerge, the scorecard will be adapted to reflect these changes and make strategy happen.

Celestica Inc.: On the Right Track

Celestica Inc. provides an excellent example of a company that appreciates the length of time setting up a scorecard initiative can take in a large organization, and has set some very realistic time frames. A world leader in electronics manufacturing services (EMS), Celestica more than tripled its net earnings in 2000 over 1999. Competing in the multi-billion-dollar electronics manufacturing services industry, fierce competition and razor-thin margins pointed to the need to look at a new way of doing business. The new mandate was to focus on one key overriding objective, to maximize its return on invested capital (ROIC).

In 1999, based on the results of other organizations and the enthusiasm of many within the company, Celestica decided that the balanced scorecard was one of the opportunities it was looking for, and moved forward with the initiative. The early mandate was to bring about awareness in the company, and to create a team that could generate enthusiasm and make inroads with the balanced scorecard. The company realized very early that, with over 39 sites worldwide, it would take a fair amount of time and effort to roll the balanced scorecard out globally. With realistic expectations to effectively deploy this initiative, the project was broken down into four phases:

1. Establish a scorecard champion and a cross-functional team, and have the team conduct studies to understand the current operational measurement process in order to effectively move forward.

2. Introduce the Balanced Scorecard concept with the Canadian operations acting as the pilot, and tie the scorecard in with corporate goals, which will be linked to and aligned with employee actions. The inception of a balanced

report card was created and communicated to the employees at large. This began the process of linking the Canadian operations measurements to corporate goals, and to employee contribution.

3. Build on the balanced structure by fine-tuning the work done to date, and continue with the linkages of employee actions to corporate goals as well as automating the data collection process.

4. Based on the work done in the pilot, roll out the scorecard system to the rest of the company globally.

The company is currently working on the completion of Phase 3. In very creative fashion, the scorecard team has decided to attack the project from two fronts. The larger team was split into two sub-teams. Sub-team A is working with the traditional approach of taking the organizational goals and translating them into lower-level action. Sub-team B is working from the "bottom" with the workers, getting their input on how they believe they could help the organization drive toward the overriding mandate of maximizing ROIC. As both activities occur simultaneously, the two co-projects will "meet in the middle", bringing closure to Phase 3.

Phase 4 is deployed as appropriate over , as it is recognized that to effectively implement these recommendations, information must be communicated quickly and continuously in order to become a cultural process — an on-going task.

The company breaks their report card into four perspectives:

1. Financial,
2. Internal,
3. Customer, and
4. People.

Each perspective is comprised of two to five measures, each of which can have its own breakdown of smaller measures. By focusing on those few factors crucial to success, the company has created a simple yet comprehensive scorecard.

The balanced scorecard is intended to play several roles at Celestica. By focusing on ROIC and its customers, the scorecard is expected to yield the following efficacies:

1. Increased ROIC — By focusing employee on-the-job requirements crucial to maximizing efficiency and minimizing invested capital (for example, inventory), ROIC will rise dramatically.

2. Increased customer satisfaction — With its own perspective and several measures focused on the customer. The customer surveys are an integral component of the Celestica feedback process.

3. Enhanced competitive advantage — By focusing employees on maximizing both ROIC and customer satisfaction, the company's competitive position will be enhanced significantly.

4. Increased employee morale — With employees empowered to strive toward corporate goals, as some of their compensation is based on the overall corporate performance, the employees will find the balanced scorecard to be an enriching experience.

As Celestica continues to develop and deploy the balanced scorecard process, all signs point toward the ability to realize the objectives. In addition, some unexpected "bonus" benefits have surfaced over the past year. For example, as the scorecard team studies and refines its measures, it has found that requests are coming from foreign sites to share their findings. In other words, as the team learns, it is sharing its findings with other divisions, thus enabling those divisions to benefit from the work done well before they become part of the formal scorecard process. In this way, it is expected that all sites will be well aware of and eager to embrace the scorecard rollout, thereby making Phase 4 a more efficient process.

So far all has gone well. However, the road to scorecard implementation has not been completely painless. During the measure automation portion of the initiative, for example, it was realized that the measures used in the report card come from a variety of sources. This was considered as an additional opportunity to improve the Data collection and reporting process. Not surprisingly, the team credits the scorecard process as the catalyst in identifying this issue.

Looking forward, Celestica continues to focus strongly on the scorecard. It will continue its efforts in refining the process already in place as it begins to roll out the scorecard to various sites internationally. By setting realistic timelines and taking an incremental approach to scorecard rollout, Celestica is poised to realize the scorecard objectives it set out initially and declare the scorecard a major success toward operational performance improvements.

Chapter 2

Strategy Formulation and the Balanced Scorecard

Overview

As mentioned in Chapter 1, the balanced scorecard is an excellent tool that can be used to translate the organizational strategy into a much more specific and meaningful performance measurement and management system. In other words, a successful balanced scorecard implementation will result in a successful strategy implementation. Employees will take action to achieve the strategy. With this in mind, it is important to consider the major role that strategy plays in this process. A good strategy coupled with a good balanced scorecard will produce desirable results. A poor strategy that utilizes a balanced scorecard can be disastrous. That said, a brief discussion on strategy formulation and its link to the balanced scorecard is merited.

Strategy Formulation

Strategy formulation can be defined as the series of steps taken in order to determine the organization's long- and short-term objectives, and the programs or strategies that will be employed in order to achieve the objectives. There is no one proper way or optimal recipe to formulate an organizational strategy. Regardless of the specific strategy formulation approach employed, a good approach will usually yield some key components:

1. A vision and/or mission statement;

2. An analysis of organizational strengths and weaknesses, as well as external opportunities and threats (commonly referred to as a SWOT analysis);

3. A set of longer-term objectives and a set of short-term objectives (the latter referred to as goals throughout this book); and

4. An action plan of some sort to achieve these objectives.

Figure 2-1 provides an illustration of the strategy formulation process above. The balanced scorecard creation process hones in on the objectives portion of the strategy, and uses this as its springboard for creation. As the balanced scorecard is usually done for a one-year period it tends to focus in on the short-term objectives (or goals) list, with the assumption that this list will have already incorporated any longer-term objectives into it. If inclusion of a longer-term objective is merited, this can be easily accommodated.

Figure 2-1: Strategy Formulation Overview

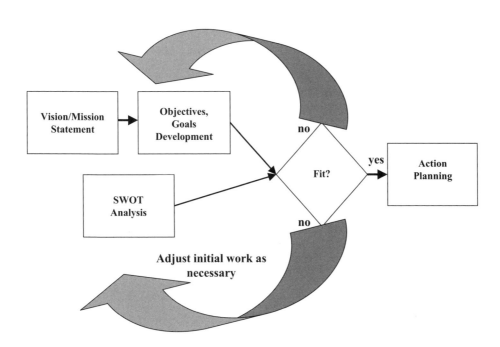

While the balanced scorecard does not necessarily directly incorporate the action plan per se, it is very closely related to the organization's action plan. As a result, it should be very consistent with the action plan. In fact, the final step in the scorecard creation process is a review for balance and completeness, at which time the action plan will be utilized for comparative purposes. Any discrepancies or inconsistencies that surface should be identified and corrected by modifying the balanced scorecard or the action plan, or both.

☞ **Formulating a "balanced strategy" can make the balanced scorecard exercise somewhat simpler. The organization can execute the strategy formulation process by defining objectives (and the subsequent goals) under the headings of the balanced scorecard perspectives. In this way, balance can be sought and ensured very early in the process, which will likely assist in the balanced scorecard implementation.**

Scorecard Goals

As indicated earlier, the creation of the balanced scorecard is possible only with a list of goals set up through the strategy formulation process (goals are defined in this book as having a one-year duration). If an organization is planning to undergo a strategy formulation process in the near future, this will provide a list of fresh and current goals that can be used for balanced scorecard creation. More likely though is the scenario where an organization has no immediate plans to re-formulate their strategy and therefore will need to do one of two things in order to provide a current set of goals:

1. Take the list of goals that were created the last time the organization underwent a strategy formulation initiative and update it; or

2. In the event that no list of goals was ever created, use the strategy to create a list of goals that can be used for balanced scorecard creation.

The resulting list of goals necessary for creation of the balanced scorecard should represent both financial and non-financial goals. In the next chapter the goals list will be screened for other criteria such as balance and completeness. At this point, as long as the list contains a relatively equal mix of both financial and non-financial goals it is sufficient for the preliminary creation of an organizational balanced scorecard.

Scorecard Goal Creation — A Simple Yet Effective Method

To this point, there has been an assumption that an organizational strategy exists from which to draw upon for the purposes of creating a list of goals. In the event that the strategy either does not exist, or has not been created in such a way as to lend itself to simple goal creation, an easy yet effective method of creating a list of goals will be provided in this section. While a full-blown strategy formulation is beyond the scope of this book, it is appropriate to add this section since goals are so important to the balanced scorecard.

There are three key steps involved in this method:

1. Define a vision for the organization;

2. Based on this vision, determine a list of 8–12 objectives; and

3. Create a list of goals based on the objectives established in Step 2.

Figure 2-2 provides an illustration of this method.

Figure 2-2: Simple Goal Creation Method

Step 1: Vision Definition

A vision can be defined as a purposefully wishful statement of where the organization could be in an ideal state five years into the future.

Vision Guidelines

A good vision statement should:

1. Be inspirational and moving;

2. Be future-oriented; and

3. Be barrier leaping.

Vision Statement Examples

The following are some real examples of strong vision statements:

1. To be a school of local and state renown, whose graduates' excellence in sporting, cultural and academic leadership is widely recognized.

2. To dominate selected markets and to become the market leader by providing the best product for the job, solid field support and continual innovation to meet customer needs.

3. To be a world leader in an extensive variety of strategic initiative workshops and implementation solutions, accessible to every organization and individual in the world, at any time.

As one can see, vision statements are generally quite succinct. There is no right or wrong vision statement, especially when it is to be used solely for the purpose of creating a list of goals for the balanced scorecard initiative.

Step 2: Creation of an Objectives List

With the vision in place, a list of 8–12 objectives should be created, aimed at fulfillment of the stated vision. An extension of the vision, the objectives list is much more tangible and is based on what the organization needs to accomplish over the next three or so years to achieve the vision.

A good objective should:

1. Start with an action word;

2. Allow one to determine whether the objective was achieved (thus determining success/failure); and

3. Answer the question "by how much" or "when", at least in a general sense.

Some examples of objectives are:

1. Create a bonus scheme linked to strategy by December 31st, 2004;

2. Achieve 20% higher levels of productivity through reengineering;

3. Reduce funds tied up in inventory by 30%; and

4. Improve customer service by 15%.

As one can see, the examples are not too specific, but are specific enough that it can be determined what if any progress there has been. Creating 8–12 objectives facilitates the next step, which is to create a list of goals based on the objectives set.

Step 3: Goal Setting

Goals are essentially a short-term translation of the objectives, covering just one year instead of three or more. A list of around 20 goals should be created from the list of objectives created in Step 2. There should be one to three goals set for each objective. Goals can also provide timelines and answer the questions "how much" and "when" for the current and next fiscal years. Specific targets can be captured in the balanced scorecard system (this will be demonstrated later in the book). Some examples of goals can be found below:

1. A 10% increase in raw material yield over 1999;

2. 15% higher profit than the industry average; and

3. A 10% increase in net income over last year.

A good goal should:

1. Address one or more of the objectives set;

2. Allow easy tracking/monitoring throughout year;

3. Be challenging but realistic and attainable; and

4. Cover a one-year time period.

Figure 2-3 provides a relational map between goals and objectives to indicate the type of goal that would be appropriate for a specific objective. Figure 2-4 provides a simple example of two goals created from a very relevant objective.

☞   **It is possible to entirely skip the strategy formulation process, and simply create a list of around 20 goals. This is not recommended, since the risk of the resulting scorecard being incomplete or unbalanced increases. However, it is better to create a scorecard without a strategy formulation than to not create a scorecard at all.**

Figure 2-3

Vision-Objectives-Goals Relational Map

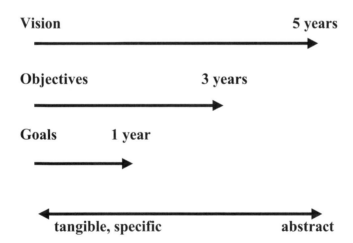

Figure 2-4: Objective-Goal Example

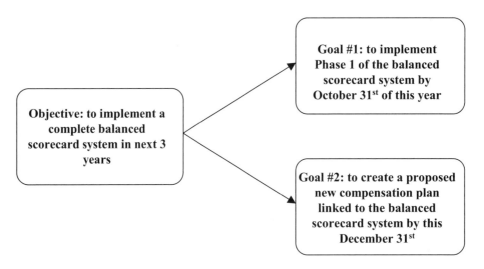

Balanced Scorecard Initiative — Delphis Mobility Demonstration

To assist in demonstrating the creation and cascade of a balanced scorecard initiative, a fictitious wireless communications organization (i.e., cell-phone service provider), Delphis Mobility, will be utilized throughout this book as a case study (please see below for a brief industry and company background). Delphis Mobility, through their strategic formulation process, has created a list of goals for the upcoming year (see Delphis Mobility's 2002 Goals List below). While a real strategy formulation should result in a list of around 20 goals, to keep the detail to a minimum for the Delphis Mobility simulation a list of 14 will be used.

Wireless Communications Industry Background

The wireless communications industry is composed of a few major players offering two main services to customers: wireless phone service and paging service. A multi-billion-dollar industry, recent years have seen margins plummet due mainly to price wars and the entry of a new low-price competitor. As a result, internal efficiencies and customer focus have become paramount in generating satisfactory returns.

Delphis Mobility History

Conceived in 1980, Delphis Mobility started slowly but gained market share and by the late 1990s was making record profits. Its best year was 1999, when revenues were $1.4 billion and after-tax profits were $114 million. The company owned 38% of the market that year. Like all the other players, the company has felt the sting of the recent price war. Early in the new millennium, the company realized that it would need to make some radical changes if it were to regain the performance it had achieved in the past. In 2001, the most recent fiscal year, market share had dropped to 29%, which resulted in revenues of $1.1 billion and after-tax profits of $88 million. The company currently has 2,500 employees.

Delphis Mobility Departments include:

1. Sales

2. Marketing

3. Customer Service

4. Information Technology (IT)

5. Network

6. Human Resources (HR)

7. Finance

phis Mobility's 2002 Goals List

- To realize after-tax profits of $110 million;

- To realize after-tax return-on-investment (ROI) of 17%;

- To increase market share to 33%;

- To reduce new-phone activation time to 12 hours;

- To increase share price to $60.00;

- To increase call range by 10%;

- To minimize the number of dropped calls;

- To realize $10 million in revenues on new service;

- To increase billing accuracy to 99.5%;

- To maximize employee satisfaction;

- To optimize the cash cycle time;

- To maximize retention of best employees;

- To maximize customer satisfaction; and

- To reduce month-end close and reporting to three days.

From this list one can see that there is a wide range of goals. In addition, the goals vary immensely in terms of specifics. Some goals give exact dollar or percentage amounts, while others are much more vague in nature. This poses no problem at all in terms of suitability for a balanced scorecard, as any detail necessary can be added later in the scorecard process. In the next chapter these goals will be used as the starting point as the Delphis Mobility balanced scorecard is created. Some will be altered slightly to make them more suitable for scorecard entry.

Summary

The importance of a strong list of strategic goals cannot be emphasized enough. Through the strategy formulation process, the organization needs to establish a list of around 20 goals that will be used as the starting point for creation of the balanced scorecard. There are many different ways to arrive at this list of goals, which will be left up to the organization to determine. One approach was discussed in this chapter, a simple yet effective method for creating the list of goals. In the next chapter the Delphis Mobility list of goals will be used in the creation of the Delphis Mobility balanced scorecard.

Chapter 3

Creating the Organization-Level Balanced Scorecard

Overview

The organization-level scorecard is the first of many phases in the complete implementation of a balanced scorecard system of performance management. From an implementation standpoint, it is the most important of all the scorecards to implement properly since it sets the tone for the entire process. Before embarking on this phase, it is appropriate to review why the organization-level scorecard is so important.

The Importance of the Organization-Level Scorecard

There are several reasons that an organization-level scorecard is important to the organization. The first reason revolves around the organizational strategy. While a sound strategy is a very important step toward organization success, it alone is insufficient. Unless there is a system in place to maximize the likelihood of strategy achievement, the risks of the organizational strategy going unfulfilled are quite high. In other words, a sound strategy is useless unless those in the organization take steps to make it happen. A balanced scorecard is a tool that can be used to reward people for taking those steps, and draw attention to those areas of the strategy that are not being fulfilled. By placing a spotlight on the critical components of the strategy, the balanced scorecard is a constant reminder to all of what the company's strategy is, and what each person needs to do to help achieve it.

Another extremely important element of the organization-level scorecard is its use later as a mechanism for creating department- and employee-level scorecards. Because of their dependence on the organization scorecard, these subsequent scorecards will only be as good as the scorecard they are derived from.

Finally, the organization-level scorecard can also be used as a component of the department-level and individual scorecards. By including the organization-level scorecard results in the cascaded scorecards, the benefits are twofold. First, it sends a message to all departments and all employees that the organization is not a set of distinct departments and employees, but rather a cohesive unit that requires everyone working together to fulfill the strategy. Second, it allows employees to share in the successes and/or failures of the organization, increasing ownership in the organization. How to integrate the organization-level scorecard into the cascaded scorecards will be discussed in subsequent chapters.

Important Considerations of Phase 1

Some important considerations in creating the organization-level scorecard are:

1. Who should actually perform the work of completing the steps?

2. How long should Phase 1 take?

3. What if we hit a roadblock?

Each of these concerns is addressed below.

ork Performance

It is highly recommended that a cross-functional team be dedicated to this phase, at least for Step 1. Ideally, someone from each department would be on this team, so that representation and input from all parties is ensured. Team members should have a very strong understanding of the organization's strategy. An external facilitator is recommended at various times throughout the project, especially at the outset of the process. The start of the exercise generally dictates the longer-term success or failure — a good start is vital.

If for some reason the team is not fully cross-functional, it is important that individuals from each department not represented be kept "in the loop", and allowed to have input on a less formal basis. The major consequence of not including all departments involved is the serious risk of a lack of ownership and buy-in by those departments that feel "out of the loop". Another consequence is the fact that, for each department not represented, there is a loss of valuable input from that area of expertise. Stated simply: the model cannot be considered complete unless representation from all areas has been included. It is crucial to include all areas on the team.

A very important consideration is that those appointed to the scorecard team need to be able to dedicate a significant amount of their time to the scorecard project, perhaps on a temporary full-time basis. It simply cannot be an "after-hours" project. If so, it is doomed to fail. There needs to be resource planning so that team members are not working on the scorecard project as well as all of their regular duties.

ration

The total period of time for the implementation of the organization scorecard can range anywhere from six months to two years, depending on several things, such as the readiness of the strategic goals (i.e., do they fit into the scorecard template?), number of goals, number of dedicated staff, and so on. Figure 3-1 provides a possible Phase 1 timeline, indicating how long each step in Phase 1 can take. These are estimates that can be used as a general guideline. A point worthy of note here is that the time to set targets and stretch goals can range quite significantly, to upward of eight months. The reason for this is that many organizations conduct benchmarking studies during this phase so that the specific goals set out have been determined against some actual reference base. This is encouraged, as long as it does not steal momentum from the balanced scorecard initiative.

☞ **A recent development in the balanced scorecard implementation field is referred to as Rapid Prototyping (RP). This concept is very useful to organizations that believe in the balanced scorecard, yet are hesitant or unable to make the time and resource commitment necessary in order to implement the system. RP essentially uses the 80/20 rule (i.e., 80% of the benefits come from the first 20% of effort) to produce a streamlined scorecard that can be produced with minimal time and effort. While a complete implementation is still recommended for thoroughness, RP can allow an organization that otherwise would not implement at all to realize most of the benefits associated with scorecard implementation. Rapid Prototyping is discussed more fully in Chapter 8.**

Figure 3-1
Phase 1 Possible Timelines

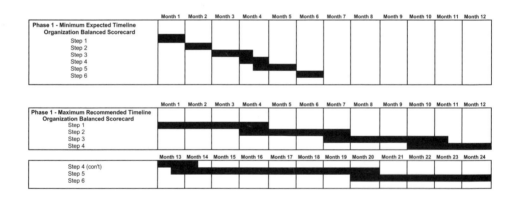

Encountering Roadblocks

Roadblocks are an unfortunate but inevitable part of any major initiative. Some typical roadblocks that will be encountered during this phase are:

- Choosing the appropriate scorecard perspective for the goals;

- Ensuring the scorecard is balanced and complete;

- Defining measures for each goal;

- Agreeing on the appropriate weights; and

● Agreeing on targets and stretch goals.

If roadblocks are encountered, it may be advisable to assign a facilitator to mediate. This could be someone from a higher level in the organization, or an outside expert in the field. The important thing to keep in mind is, balanced scorecard implementation is a long process — minor roadblocks should not be allowed to become the causes of major delay.

ase 1: The Step-by-Step View

The major initiative of this phase of the balanced scorecard is to create a balanced scorecard that will represent the desired direction of the entire organization. This is a significant undertaking, and is best achieved by breaking the phase down into the following steps:

1. Categorize and place each of the goals created earlier into the balanced-scorecard template;

2. Review for balance, and adjust where necessary;

3. Determine how each goal will be measured;

4. Assign weights to each perspective, and each goal;

5. Set targets and stretch goals; and

6. Review for balance and completeness.

Figure 3-2 provides a pictorial view of the entire Phase 1 process.

Figure 3-2
Phase 1 Overview

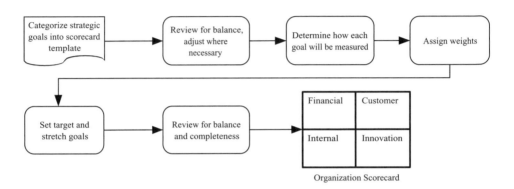

Organization Scorecard

Step 1: Categorizing Goals

At this point, it is assumed that the mapping process emphasized in Chapter 2 has been completed, and a list of around 20 goals exists. The focus of this step then is to take those goals and determine which of the four scorecard perspectives they relate to the most. Making this determination in some cases will be fairly obvious. For example, a goal of "Maximize after-tax profits" is clearly a financial goal — it fits much better in the financial perspective than in any of customer, internal business, or innovation and learning.

Many goals will not be as simple to categorize, and judgment will need to be used. For example, a stated goal might be "Reduce defects by 10%". This could be argued for either of two perspectives — customer or internal business. Some would say that defect reduction is achieved by changing internal business processes and thus belongs in this perspective. Others would suggest that defect reduction is an improvement in quality that benefits customers, so it belongs in the customer perspective. Interestingly, they are both right. With goals of this nature, there is rarely any right or wrong with respect to perspective categorization — the one that creates the higher level of comfort and buy-in is the right one (which is why both schools of thought above are correct). The one caveat here is to avoid categorizing all of these types of goals into one perspective, as this may give the illusion that a scorecard is unbalanced, when in fact it is fairly balanced.

While there are no hard and fast rules for goal categorization, some general rules of thumb for the categorization process can be used. First, it is wise to go through the list and categorize the most obvious goals first. Goals like the profit goal example above are usually quite easy to gain agreement on, and can serve as a quick momentum builder. The most obvious goals will then have been categorized, leaving a shorter list of less obvious goals. For Delphis Mobility, the following goals seem obvious enough that they can be categorized immediately:

- To realize after-tax profits of $110 million (financial);

- To realize after-tax return-on-investment (ROI) of 17% (financial);

- To increase share price to $60.00 (financial);

- To increase market share to 33% (customer);

- To maximize employee satisfaction (innovation and learning);

- To optimize the cash cycle time (financial);

- To maximize retention of best employees (innovation and learning);

- To maximize customer satisfaction (customer); and

- To reduce month-end close and reporting to three days (internal business process).

So from the original list of 14 goals, nine have been categorized and five less obvious goals remain to be categorized. Figure 3-3 shows the partially completed scorecard summary page constructed to this point. Some of the goals represented at this point on the balanced scorecard have had the specific financial and numerical targets taken out. The reason for this is that in Step 6, target and stretch goals are added onto another sheet. At this point in the scorecard process, specific financial and numerical targets are not necessary; a summary format is sufficient.

Figure 3-3
Delphis Mobility
Partial Balanced Scorecard Summary
Fiscal 2002

Financial		*Customer*	
Goals	**Measures**	**Goals**	**Measures**
Maximize after-tax profits		Maximize market share	
Maximize ROI		Maximize customer satisfaction	
Minimize cash cycle time			
Maximize share price			
Internal Business Process		*Innovation & Learning*	
Goals	**Measures**	**Goals**	**Measures**
Reduce month end close and reporting cycle time		Maximize employee satisfaction ratio	
		Maximize retention of best employees	

The scorecard appears unbalanced at this point. However, no effort should be put into balancing the scorecard until all goals have been categorized and entered into the scorecard. A couple of techniques for categorizing the remaining goals will be demonstrated below.

The first categorization technique that can be used for less obvious goals is to eliminate any perspectives that clearly do not apply. For example, for the goal "To reduce new phone activation time to 12 hours", simple logic will allow the elimination of two perspectives. First, there is no financial orientation to this goal, which rules out the financial perspective. Second, there is no real orientation toward innovation or learning, which rules out this perspective. This narrows the list down to two perspectives. A reduced activation window will require some internal business changes. However in this case, the changes are minor. In other words, internal business processes do not need to be re-engineered in order to accommodate this goal. So a case could be made for placing this goal in the internal business perspective. Since a 12-hour activation of a new phone is very visible to a customer who tries using the phone 12 hours after subscribing, a case can also be made for entering the goal in the customer perspective. Add the fact that a recent customer survey suggests that potential customers would use activation time as a criterion in choosing a carrier, and a very strong case can be made for inclusion in the customer perspective. So using company and industry knowledge allowed the goal to be categorized where it "best" fits (i.e., not the "only" place it fits).

Eiminating certain perspectives can be useful in reducing the number of potential choices. From there, it is easier to determine which perspective is likely the most appropriate. This will assist in categorizing many of the remaining goals, leaving hopefully just a few that will require further analysis. Any goals not categorized after the technique above has been attempted should be categorized using the next technique.

Any goals still remaining at this point are clearly the more ambiguous goals, more difficult than the others in determining the most appropriate perspective. These goals should therefore be analyzed by asking some or all of the following questions:

- Is the goal focused on revenue, profits or return on investment? If yes, this is likely a financial perspective goal.

- Is the goal one where the customer will see the results (directly or indirectly) in the shorter term (i.e., within one year)? If yes, this is likely a customer perspective goal.

- Does the goal focus on internal process improvement, where the results are virtually invisible to most customers in the shorter term? If yes, this is likely an internal business process perspective goal.

- Is the goal focused on attainment of new skills and/or knowledge, or is the goal employee-focused? If yes, this is likely an innovation and learning perspective goal.

Usually by asking these questions the choice can be narrowed down to two possible perspectives. In this case, simply choose the perspective with the fewer goals. At this point in the process it is simply not worth the additional effort of further analysis. It is more important to keep the momentum going. Adjustments can be made at a later time if deemed appropriate.

☞ **Remember, a balanced scorecard that is 80% balanced is still better than any alternative performance measurement system. Do NOT strive for perfection — there is no such thing with a balanced scorecard implementation. Instead, seek the best possible solution. Later, during the process improvement phase, improvements can be made based on new knowledge and lessons learned.**

For the Delphis Mobility goals that have not to this point been categorized, the rationale for the categorization found in Figure 3-4 is as follows. First, the goal "To reduce new phone activation time to 12 hours" has been entered into the customer perspective, for reasons discussed earlier. Second, the goal "To increase call range by 10%" has been entered into the internal business process perspective. This could easily have been placed into the customer perspective, since increasing call range is for customers. It was placed into the internal business process perspective since there are several internal processes that must be undertaken to increase the call range, all of which are invisible to the customer until the day the call range increases. In addition, the increase in call range is not expected to be visible to most customers, just those in certain peripheral areas. Therefore a judgment call was made to include it in the internal business process perspective.

Figure 3-4
Delphis Mobility
Partial Balanced Scorecard Summary
Fiscal 2002

Financial			Customer		
Goals		**Measures**	**Goals**		**Measures**
Maximize after-tax profits			Maximize market share		
Maximize ROI			Maximize customer satisfaction		
Minimize cash cycle time			Reduce new phone activation time		
Maximize share price					
Internal Business Process			**Innovation & Learning**		
Goals		**Measures**	**Goals**		**Measures**
Reduce month end close and reporting cycle time			Maximize employee satisfaction ratio		
Increase call range			Maximize retention of best employees		
Minimize number of dropped calls			Maximize new billable service revenues		
Maximize billing accuracy					

The next goal to be categorized is "To minimize the number of dropped calls". This has been entered into the internal business process perspective, for reasons similar to the goal "To increase call range by 10%" discussed above. While ultimately customers will be the beneficiaries of a reduced number of dropped phone calls, in the shorter term most of the effort expended will focus on improving internal business processes. The next goal, "To increase billing accuracy to 99.5%", has also been entered into the internal business process perspective since it will require internal business improvements in the shorter term to reach this goal. Finally, the goal "To realize $10 million in revenues on new service offerings" has been entered into the innovation and learning perspective. While the dollar amount may lend itself to the financial perspective, the fact is that in order to generate revenue on new service offerings, new services must be developed which require both learning and innovation.

p 2: Reviewing the Scorecard for Balance

At this point each goal from the strategy goal list should be contained in the balanced scorecard. It is now time to review the contents of the balanced scorecard, checking for balance and completeness. Of course, any shortcomings cited should have the appropriate adjustments made.

The check for balance can be done first. The questions that should be asked are:

- Are there four to seven goals per perspective?

- Within any perspective, are most or all the goals biased or weighted toward just one dimension of that perspective?

- Has any important element of the organization (employees, for example) been overlooked?

- Does it seem to be balanced?

Answering these questions will be helpful in determining the overall balance of the balanced scorecard. The last question is an important one. One can apply as many rules as exist in creating a balanced scorecard, but instincts or "gut feel" are also important. The scorecard should seem balanced to the creators — it should feel right.

Turning once again to Figure 3-4, it is clear that both the customer perspective and the innovation and learning perspective each have just three goals. They will need at least one more each for the scorecard to be considered balanced. Assume that after revisiting the strategy, the company realized that a customer goal that should be evident is the reduction of churn (or lost customers). Therefore it seems like a natural fit to add this to the customer perspective of the scorecard. Another initiative the company wants to emphasize in 2002 is a better skill set in project management. It would seem then, that adding a project management-related goal to the innovation and learning perspective is appropriate.

With an acceptable number of goals in each perspective, it is important at this point to ensure that there is no bias toward any one dimension. Also, a review to see if anything has been overlooked is also appropriate. For Delphis Mobility, it appears that everything is in balance. Figure 3-5 shows the balanced scorecard summary page for Delphis Mobility with a complete and balanced set of goals (this simulation will use the minimum amount of goals necessary to satisfy the guidelines — in a real implementation scenario a total list of goals closer to 20 or 25 would be expected).

Figure 3-5
Delphis Mobility
Partial Balanced Scorecard Summary
Fiscal 2002

Financial			*Customer*		
Goals	**Measures**		**Goals**	**Measures**	
Maximize after-tax profits			Maximize market share		
Maximize ROI			Maximize customer satisfaction		
Minimize cash cycle time			Reduce new phone activation time		
Maximize share price			Minimize 'churn' (lost customer) rate		
Internal Business Process			*Innovation & Learning*		
Goals	**Measures**		**Goals**	**Measures**	
Reduce month end close and reporting cycle time			Maximize employee satisfaction ratio		
Increase call range			Maximize retention of best employees		
Minimize number of dropped calls			Maximize new billable service revenues		
Maximize billing accuracy			Increase number of employees certified in project management		

 There is empirical evidence to suggest that roughly ¹/₃ of the goals are found in the internal business perspective (i.e., for a balanced scorecard organization that has 24 goals, about eight will be found in this perspective). The remaining goals are distributed fairly evenly across the remaining perspectives.

Step 3: Determining Measures

With the goal portion of the scorecard now complete, it is time to determine the measure(s) most applicable for each goal. It is measures that will facilitate the actual scoring of the scorecard later, necessary to determine whether and to what degree goals were achieved. The best way to determine the most appropriate measure(s) for a goal is to ask the question, "At the end of the fiscal period, what set of information will best indicate whether the goal was achieved?" The answer to this question will likely provide the best measure.

In many cases, the appropriate measure will be fairly obvious. For example, for the goal "To realize after-tax return-on-investment (ROI)", the appropriate measure is clearly the actual ROI. In other cases the best measure will not be quite as straightforward. A good example is "To maximize retention of best employees", a goal for which an obvious measure is not readily apparent. Since measure determination is a crucial aspect at the departmental and individual levels as well as the organization level, a complete discussion on this topic is found in Chapter 7.

Figure 3-6 provides a partial balanced scorecard summary page, complete with goals and their corresponding measures.

Figure 3-6
Delphis Mobility
Partial Balanced Scorecard Summary
Fiscal 2002

Financial		Customer	
Goals	**Measures**	**Goals**	**Measures**
Maximize after-tax profits	Actual after-tax profits ($M)	Maximize market share	Actual market share %
Maximize ROI	Actual ROI (%)	Maximize customer satisfaction	Customer satisfaction index results
Minimize cash cycle time	Average number of receivable days	Reduce new phone activation time	Average actual new phone activation time (hours)
Maximize share price	Actual share price	Minimize 'churn' (lost customer) rate	Actual churn rate

Internal Business Process		Innovation & Learning	
Goals	**Measures**	**Goals**	**Measures**
Reduce month end close and reporting cycle time	Actual month end close and reporting time (days)	Maximize employee satisfaction ratio	Actual employee satisfaction ratio
Increase call range	Actual increase in call range	Maximize retention of best employees	Actual average number of employee years with company
Minimize number of dropped calls	Actual dropped call percentage	Maximize new billable service revenues	Actual revenues from new billable services ($M)
Maximize billing accuracy	Actual billing accuracy percentage	Increase number of employees certified in project management	Actual percentage of employees certified in project management

p 4: Assigning Weights

The weighting exercise is a very crucial component of the balanced scorecard initiative. It is with weights that a very strong message can be sent regarding the relative importance of each goal and perspective. The weighting can have a dramatic effect on the overall scorecard score, since final scores are determined by multiplying by the relative weight (this will be demonstrated shortly). There are actually two weighting exercises that must take place. The first is the weighting of the four perspectives. The other is the weighting of goals within each perspective.

It is incorrect to assume that, since there are four perspectives, each should get an equal (i.e., 25% weighting). It is only in very rare instances that this would be appropriate. Instead, the weighting used should reflect the strategy chosen by the organization. For example, an organization that has chosen a strategy with a differentiation or innovation theme is going to put extra weighting on the innovation and learning perspective. Conversely, an organization following a cost leadership strategy will place more weighting on the internal business perspective.

Generally speaking, the customer perspective should always be weighted proportionately higher (i.e., greater than 25%), while the financial perspective should always be weighted proportionately lower (i.e., less than 25%). Why is this? First, the financial perspective should be weighted lower since it is an outcome-based perspective. In other words, the organization controls the results of this perspective only by the actions taken in the other three perspectives. For example, take the goal "To maximize ROI". This can only be achieved by actions taken in the other perspectives (e.g., maximizing customer satisfaction). Since the weighting is used to point the organization to where effort should be expended, it is only logical that most of the weighting be focused on non-outcomes-based perspectives.

One may wonder then, why the financial perspective weighting would not be zero. The answer: fiscal responsibility. While it is great to focus on strategy and take actions that will maximize long-term success, the fact still remains that every organization must also survive and prosper in the short run in order to make it to the long term. The financial perspective assists in providing the information to ensure short-run prosperity, and acts as a "check" against whether the chosen strategy is actually assisting the company in achieving its financial goals. De-emphasizing this too much send the wrong message.

The customer perspective should always be weighted proportionately higher since the customer perspective is really the focal point of the balanced scorecard. Both the internal business and innovation and learning perspectives exist to ultimately optimize the customer perspective. The financial perspective is largely determined by the results of the customer perspective. Therefore this perspective merits more weighting.

In determining the final weighting for each perspective, it is important to acknowledge the fact that tradeoffs need to be made. It is interesting when people are asked to weight the individual perspectives how often the total is greater than 100%. It is sometimes difficult but always necessary to realize that, for each percentage point one perspective is given, another must do without. Figure 3-7 provides a possible perspective weighting for Delphis Mobility.

Figure 3-7
Delphis Mobility
Balanced Scorecard Weighting Summary
2002

	Weighting
Financial	20%
Customer	35%
Internal Business Process	25%
Innovation & Learning	20%
Total Weighting (must = 100%)	100%

Next, the goals within each perspective must be assigned weights. To facilitate this, a supplementary schedule must be used that allows for additional detail. Figure 3-8 provides a schedule that allows weights to be entered for each goal of Delphis Mobility's financial perspective. Not surprisingly, the weights within each perspective must add to exactly 100%. This way, goals within each perspective can be ranked based on their relative importance. Figures 3-9, 3-10 and 3-11 provide the weighted goals for the customer, internal business process and innovation and learning perspectives, respectively.

> ☞ **Weights should be expected to vary over time, as circumstances and strategies change. An organization should review the weighting structure at least annually and even during the fiscal period when appropriate, especially in the first year of implementation.**

Figure 3-8
Delphis Mobility
Financial Perspective
2002

Goals	Weight	Measures
Maximize after-tax profits	25%	Actual after-tax profits ($M)
Maximize ROI	35%	Actual ROI (%)
Minimize cash cycle time	15%	Average number of receivable days
Maximize share price	25%	Actual share price
Total Weight (must = 100%)	**100%**	

Figure 3-9
Delphis Mobility
Customer Perspective
2002

Goals	Weight	Measures
Maximize market share	30%	Actual market share %
Maximize customer satisfaction	30%	Customer satisfaction index results
Reduce new phone activation time	20%	Average actual new phone activation time (hours)
Minimize 'churn' (lost customer) rate	20%	Actual churn rate
Total Weight (must = 100%)	**100%**	

Figure 3-10
Delphis Mobility
Internal Business Process Perspective
2002

Goals	Weight	Measures
Reduce month end close and reporting cycle time	25%	Actual month end close and reporting time (days)
Increase call range	20%	Actual increase in call range
Minimize number of dropped calls	30%	Actual dropped call percentage
Maximize billing accuracy	25%	Actual billing accuracy percentage
Total Weight (must = 100%)	**100%**	

Figure 3-11
Delphis Mobility
Innovation & Learning Perspective
2002

Goals	*Weight*	*Measures*
Maximize employee satisfaction ratio	30%	Actual employee satisfaction ratio
Maximize retention of best employees	25%	Actual average number of employee years with company
Maximize new billable service revenues	30%	Actual revenues from new billable services ($M)
Increase number of employees certified in project management	15%	Actual percentage of employees certified in project management
Total Weight (must = 100%)	**100%**	

ep 5: Setting Target and Stretch Goals

The next step in creating the balanced scorecard is to add target and stretch goals. A target goal can be loosely defined as a desired result that, if achieved, will make the organization pleased. A stretch goal on the other hand, is a desired result that will make the organization extremely pleased.

Earlier in the chapter it was recommended that any specific components of goals, such as dollar figures or percentages, be removed for the summary page. The reason for this is twofold. First, it provides for a succinct one-page balanced scorecard summary that is not too detailed. This detail will be readily viewable in a supplementary sheet. Also, there is a risk in providing just one specific target in that it can create complacency in the event of a perception that the goal is very easy to attain. For example, take the targeted ROI of 17%. If at some point during the fiscal period it becomes clear to employees that this goal can and will easily be reached, people may begin to "coast" for a couple of reasons: first, because they may feel that they deserve to coast (after all, they will reach the target set forth by management) and second, since future targets will likely be based on actual results, an employee may just be setting themselves up to have the bar raised in the near future.

To avoid this scenario, it is highly recommended that a stretch goal be created with targets, so that there is almost always some motivation to work toward optimizing the goals put forth. Stretch goals should be created such that they are very difficult to achieve, but finishing somewhere in between target and stretch is realistic with dedication and hard work. This will keep employees motivated to continue striving toward goal optimization even in the event of a realization that the target will be surpassed.

Target and stretch goals must be as specific and measurable as possible. Figure 3-12 provides target and stretch goals for Delphis Mobility's financial perspective. Figures 3-13, 3-14 and 3-15 provide the target and stretch goals for the customer, internal business process and innovation and learning perspectives, respectively. In some cases, the target in the scorecard may be different from that stated during the strategy formulation process. For example, the strategy stated a targeted market share of 33%. In reality, however, management may be pleased with an actual result of 32%, while hoping for 33% or even more. The target-stretch combination affords the ability to set a target lower than that stated in the strategy, since the stretch will be higher. This way, employees can be given realistic targets and still be motivated to surpass them.

Figure 3-12
Delphis Mobility
Financial Perspective
2002

Goals	Weight	Measures	Target	Stretch
Maximize after-tax profits	25%	Actual after-tax profits ($M)	$ 110.0	$ 130.0
Maximize ROI	35%	Actual ROI (%)	17%	19%
Minimize cash cycle time	15%	Average number of receivable days	45	40
Maximize share price	25%	Actual share price	$ 60.00	$ 75.00
Total Weight (must = 100%)	**100%**			

Step 6: Review for Balance and Completeness

The final step in Phase 1 is to review the entire balanced scorecard for balance and completeness. While the initial check for balance was completed much earlier, it is possible that the circumstances (either internal or external) might have changed that would call for adjustments to the scorecard. For example, changing trends in customer expectation might necessitate the need to change or add another customer-focused goal. Or a mandate toward innovation may prompt a decision to add weighting to the innovation and learning perspective. An important principle that should always be kept in mind is flexibility. Until the scorecard is complete and published it is a work in process, and should be communicated as such. It is important not to set the scorecard in stone too early, if at all.

During the first year or two of the scorecard implementation, it may be wise to allow for changes as necessary as part of the learning process. This may assist in gaining employee buy-in. For example, if a competitor launches an unexpected service that clearly threatens the market share expectations, it may be wise to adjust these down. Otherwise, the scorecard may be associated with unrealistic expectations and poor bonuses that could be devastating in terms of employee acceptance.

Figure 3-13
Delphis Mobility
Customer Perspective
2002

Goals	Weight	Measures	Target	Stretch
Maximize market share	30%	Actual market share %	32.0%	36.0%
Maximize customer satisfaction	30%	Customer satisfaction index results	85%	90%
Reduce new phone activation time	20%	Average actual new phone activation time (hours)	13	11
Minimize 'churn' (lost customer) rate	20%	Actual churn rate	2.0%	1.6%

Total Weight (must = 100%) | **100%**

Figure 3-14
Delphis Mobility
Internal Business Process Perspective
2002

Goals	Weight	Measures	Target	Stretch
Reduce month end close and reporting cycle time	25%	Actual month end close and reporting time (days)	3.5	3.0
Increase call range	20%	Actual increase in call range	8%	12%
Minimize number of dropped calls	30%	Actual dropped call percentage	2%	1%
Maximize billing accuracy	25%	Actual billing accuracy percentage	99.2%	99.7%

Total Weight (must = 100%) | **100%**

Figure 3-15
Delphis Mobility
Innovation and Learning Perspective
2002

Goals	Weight	Measures	Target	Stretch
Maximize employee satisfaction ratio	30%	Actual employee satisfaction ratio	84%	90%
Maximize retention of best employees	25%	Actual average number of employee years with company	2.5	2.8
Maximize new billable service revenues	30%	Actual revenues from new billable services ($M)	$ 9.5	$ 11.0
Increase number of employees certified in project management	15%	Actual percentage of employees certified in project management	20%	25%
Total Weight (must = 100%)	**100%**			

Summary

At this point the organization scorecard phase is complete. The process is not, however. It is very important at this point to communicate the scorecard through the organization. There should also be some mechanism for employees to ask questions and voice concerns. Effective change management, discussed later in the book, is crucial to the success of the scorecard initiative. It is strongly recommended that change management techniques be employed wherever applicable.

The next crucial step is to cascade the scorecard down one level to the departments of the organization. This is the subject of the next chapter.

Chapter 4

The Departmental-Level Cascade

Overview

With the organization-level scorecard complete, it is now appropriate to begin the process of cascading, or rolling out, the scorecard to the existing departments. Before embarking on this phase, it is appropriate to review why the cascade process is so important.

 While the term "department" is used here, the concepts apply also to teams or groups that have been created. If there are teams or groups in the organization, the concepts in this chapter apply to them as well as to departments.

The Importance of the Departmental Cascade Phase

While an organizational-level scorecard is a great accomplishment, the truth is, most employees will not be able to relate to most of its large scope and impact. The main reason for this is that, done properly, its coverage is quite comprehensive and as such will contain several parameters that most employees won't be able to fully comprehend. Being focused in one department, the "big picture" is not usually part of the regular routine for most employees. Evidence indicates that it is difficult to evaluate departmental employees with an organizational scorecard, mainly because there are simply too many items that do not apply to these individuals' responsibilities and that are out of their direct control. Evaluating people on measures that they cannot control is both difficult and inappropriate. Instead, it is wiser to make the scorecard implementation more understandable and relatable to employees. The cascade process is appropriate for this.

 Cascading the balanced scorecard is very useful for sending ownership down the ranks of the organization to the employees who actually do most of the work. Communicating "what" is expected as the balanced scorecard allows employees at lower levels to take control of "how" they intend to achieve scorecard results. This is also consistent with the concept of employee empowerment.

Important Considerations of Phase 2

Some important considerations in performing the department cascade process are:

1. Who should actually perform the work of completing these steps?

2. How long should Phase 2 take?

3. What if we hit a roadblock?

Each of these concerns is addressed below.

▶rk Performance

It is highly recommended that a cross-functional team be dedicated to this phase, at least for Step 1. Ideally, someone from each department would be on this team, so that representation and input from all parties is ensured. An external facilitator is recommended at various times throughout the project, especially at the outset of the cascade process. The start of the exercise generally dictates the longer-term success or failure — a good start is vital.

If for some reason the team is not fully cross-functional, it is important that individuals from each department not represented be kept "in the loop", and allowed to have input on a less formal basis. The major consequence of not including all departments involved is the serious risk of a lack of ownership and buy-in by those departments that feel "out of the loop". Another consequence is the fact that, for each department not represented, there is a loss of valuable input from that area of expertise. Stated simply: the model cannot be considered complete unless representation from all areas has been included. It is crucial to include all areas on the team.

A very important consideration is that those appointed to the scorecard team need to be able to dedicate a significant amount of their time to the scorecard project, ideally on a full-time basis. It simply cannot be an "after-hours" project. If so, it is doomed to fail. There needs to be resource planning so that team members are not working on the scorecard project as well as all of their regular duties.

Once steps one to three are complete, it is possible for each department to assume responsibility for their own scorecard. Another option is to keep the team in charge throughout the entire cascade process. The specific organizational circumstances should dictate which is most appropriate. No matter what approach is taken, it is imperative to have a project owner responsible for monitoring departmental progress and taking action where necessary. If just one department falls behind, the entire project could be delayed. It is crucial to have someone stay on top of this.

▶ation

The total period of time for the implementation of Phase 2 can range anywhere from three months to one year, depending on several things — the number of departments, number of scorecard goals, number of dedicated staff, and so on. Figure 4-1 provides a possible Phase 2 timeline, indicating how long each step in Phase 2 can take. These are estimates that can be used as a general guideline.

Figure 4-1
Phase 2 Possible Timelines

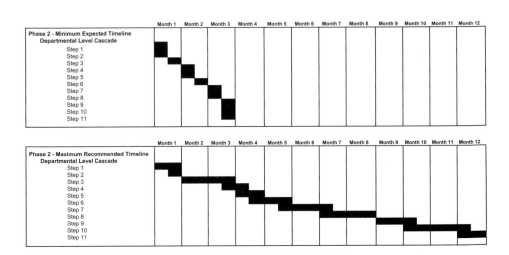

Encountering Roadblocks

Roadblocks are an unfortunate but inevitable part of any major initiative. Some typical roadblocks that will be encountered during this phase are:

- Determining the materiality of a department's impact;
- Determining the complete set of key performance factors (KPFs);
- Choosing the appropriate scorecard perspective for the goals;
- Defining measures for each goal;
- Agreeing on the appropriate weights; and
- Agreeing on targets and stretch goals.

If roadblocks are encountered, it may be advisable to assign a facilitator to mediate. This could be someone from a higher level in the organization, or an outside expert in the field. The important thing to keep in mind is, balanced scorecard implementation is a long process — minor roadblocks should not be allowed to become the causes of major delay.

Phase 2: The Step-by-Step View

The major initiative of this phase of the cascading process is to create a balanced scorecard for each department, using the organizational scorecard as the blueprint or guide. This is a significant undertaking, and is best achieved by breaking the phase down into the following steps:

1. For each organizational scorecard goal, determine the departments that have a material impact;

2. Re-organize the results from the first step into departmental summaries;

3. Those departments identified, determine what the specific impact(s) on the goal are (KPFs);

4. Organize the KPFs into one list, eliminating duplicates;

5. Re-phrase the KPFs into departmental goals;

6. Categorize the departmental goals into the four balanced scorecard perspectives;

7. Add any other appropriate goals;

8. Determine how each goal will be measured;

9. Assign weights to each perspective, and each goal;

10. Set targets and stretch goals; and

11. Review for balance and completeness.

Figure 4-2 provides a pictorial view of the entire Phase 2 process.

Figure 4-2
Phase 2 Overview

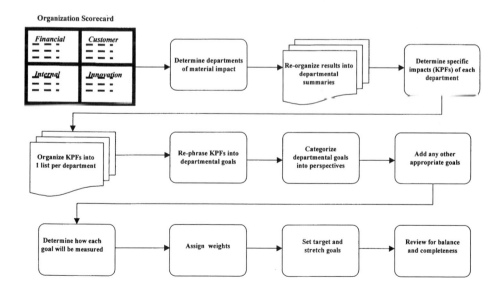

Step 1: Determining the Departments of Material Impact

In this step, the organizational scorecard is reviewed, goal by goal, to determine the departments that have a material impact on each goal. The term "material" can have many interpretations. In this case, consider material to mean that the impact of the department on the goal in question is significant enough to merit the additional administrative work required to track and measure it on a scorecard. This is a judgement call. If unsure whether a department's impact is material, or there is debate about it, it is advisable to include it as material. If at a later time it is deemed immaterial, or the department's scorecard becomes too complex, it can be eliminated.

During this step, it is not imperative to identify exactly how a department impacts a goal. In fact, this level of detail is discouraged, since it can slow the progress of this step. Instead, the main objective should be to identify all departments having a material impact. Often this will be very obvious. For example, for the goal of maximizing customer satisfaction, it is pretty obvious that the Customer Service Department has a large impact. Similarly, for the goal of profit maximization, the contribution of Sales is fairly evident. Sometimes the impact is less obvious, and more thought needs to go into determining whether the department has material impact. Any notes taken when determining whether a department does have a material impact should be kept for the next stage. Due to the fact that there will be many goals to go through, and many departments to identify, it is advisable to keep the analysis at a high level during this step, saving the detailed analysis for subsequent steps.

It is important during this step to take a straightforward approach that everyone can understand. One possibility is referred to as a "fishbone" view, where the scorecard goal is put at the front arrow, and all departments having a material impact are listed. Figure 4-3 provides an illustrated view of the fishbone method for two of the organizational scorecard goals. Many people find that the pictorial view is useful in keeping clear which departments impact which goals. This process continues for each scorecard goal until all departments having material impact have been identified. This step can be considered complete once each goal has had an impact analysis done. Once complete, there will be a "fishbone" for each goal. Table 4-1 summarizes the departments impacting each goal for Delphis Mobility after the impact determination has been performed on all goals in the organizational scorecard.

Figure 4-3
Delphis Mobility
Departmental Impact Analysis — Pictorial View

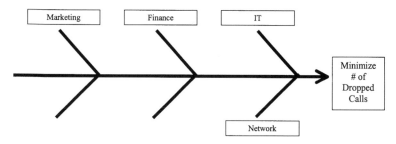

Goal: Minimize Number of Dropped Calls

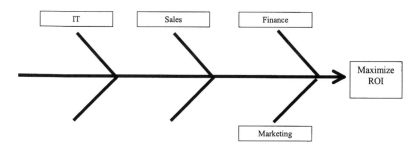

Goal: Maximize ROI

Table 4-1 *Goal/Department Impact Summary*	
Goals	Departments of Impact
1. Maximize after-tax profits	Finance, Sales, Marketing, IT, Network, HR, Customer Service
2. Maximize ROI	Finance, Sales, Marketing, IT, Network, HR, Customer Service
3. Minimize cash cycle time	Finance
4. Maximize share price	Finance, Sales, Marketing, IT, Network, HR, Customer Service
5. Maximize market share	Finance, Sales, Marketing, IT, Network, Customer Service
6. Maximize customer satisfaction	Finance, Sales, Marketing, IT, Network, HR, Customer Service

Goals	Departments of Impact
7. Reduce new phone activation time	IT, Customer Service
8. Minimize churn rate	Sales, Marketing, IT, Network
9. Reduce month end close and reporting cycle time	Finance
10. Increase call range	Finance, Sales, Marketing, Network
11. Minimize number of dropped calls	Network
12. Maximize billing accuracy	IT, Customer Service
13. Maximize job satisfaction ratio	HR
14. Maximize retention of best employees	HR
15. Increase new billable services revenue	Sales, Marketing, IT
16. Increase number of employees certified in project management	HR

Step 2: Reorganization of Analysis Results into Departmental Summaries

At this point, there are a number of departments that have been identified for the many goals in the organizational scorecard. It is possible to reorganize the information by splitting off the departments from one another, and forming a summary for each department. Figure 4-4 provides a graphical representation of this reorganization process. In an actual implementation, this would be done for each department. IT will be the department used to simulate the cascade process throughout this chapter, so only it will be followed here forward. Please see the box insert for a brief description of the IT Department's role at Delphis Mobility.

Figure 4-4
Reorganizing KPF Results

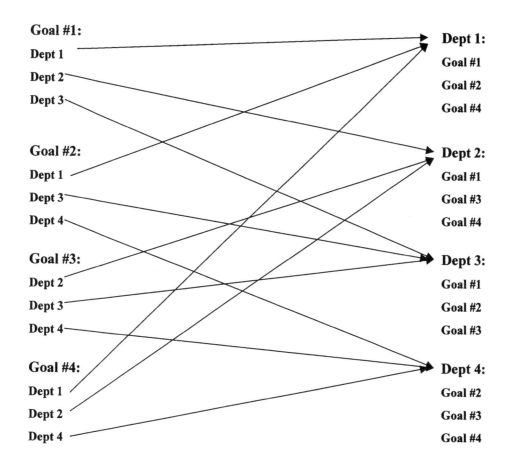

Department

The IT Department currently has a staff of 320 employees. Like other IT departments in the wireless communications industry, Delphis Mobility's IT Department is charged with the following strategic tasks:

- Collecting and storing all relevant information pertaining to customers and transactions;

- Monthly billing;

- Developing new billable services in conjunction with Marketing;

- Maintaining and improving the integrated voice response (i.e., Press 1 for ...) system; and

- Activating new subscriber phones in conjunction with Customer Service.

In the competitive landscape of wireless communications, most support departments like IT are being asked to do more with less. All departments at Delphis Mobility will have their own scorecard cascaded from the organizational scorecard as part of the scorecard implementation, including IT.

Table 4-2 provides a department goal impact summary for IT.

Table 4-2   *IT Goal Impact Summary*
1. Maximize after-tax profits
2. Maximize ROI
4. Maximize share price
5. Maximize market share
6. Maximize customer satisfaction
7. Reduce new phone activation time
8. Minimize churn rate
12. Maximize billing accuracy
15. Increase new billable services revenue

Step 3: Key Performance Factor Analysis

Now that each department has been neatly organized around the specific goals it impacts, the next step is to perform a more detailed analysis on each department about how the department specifically impacts the goal(s) identified. In performing this analysis exercise, the main question that needs to be asked for each goal identified is "for this goal, what does this department need to do to assist in achieving the goal?" The answer to this question can be referred to as a key performance factor, or KPF. KPFs can be defined as those actions that will assist the organization in achieving its stated goal(s), and are stated as an action. For example, a department KPF for the goal of profit maximization could be to demonstrate strong fiscal constraint in technology purchases.

A couple more points regarding KPFs merit discussion. First, there can, and often will, be more than one KPF for a given goal. It is important to identify all KPFs related to a goal — otherwise, the risk of an incomplete scorecard increases. Second, generally speaking, the lower down in the organization the cascading process goes, the more specific and operational the KPFs will become. This will be demonstrated in the next chapter, discussing the cascade at the individual level. At the department level, the KPFs can be described as somewhat general.

This KPF exercise requires a great amount of brainstorming, and should include the input of knowledgeable people across several areas of the organization. For Delphis Mobility's IT Department, a brainstorming session should result in a list of items like that found in Figure 4-5, which is called a KPF Summary Document. Note that in Figure 4-5, several of the KPFs are found to apply to more than one goal. For example, the KPF "demonstrating strong fiscal constraint in technology purchases" is identified for several goals, including:

- Maximize after-tax profits;

- Maximize ROI; and

- Maximize share price.

Note that there is a column to the far right entitled "Significance". It is recommended that this column be used to indicate the degree of significance of the KPF on the goal: high, medium, or low. This will help later when assigning weights. Generally speaking, the lower the level of significance, the smaller the weight the KPF will be. When a KPF is common across two or more goals, the degree of significance of the KPF can be different depending on the goal. For example, the KPF "Create and develop new and marketable services" was given a medium rating for the goal "Maximize ROI", given the relatively minor contribution new services makes toward overall ROI. However, the same KPF was given a high rating for the goal "Increase New Service Revenue", since it clearly has a much higher impact on this goal. It is common to have different significance ratings for different goals, and having this information will help in the weighting exercise.

Figure 4-5
Delphis Mobility
Balanced Scorecard
Department KPF Summary

Department: IT *Goal 1: Maximize After-Tax Profits* *Key Performance Factors*	*Significance (h/m/l)*
Demonstrate strong fiscal constraint in technology purchases	h
Demonstrate strong fiscal constraint in hiring procedures	h
Create and develop new and marketable services	m
Provide the systems to ensure timely, accurate reporting for decision-making purposes	h

Goal 2: Maximize ROI Key Performance Factors	Significance (h/m/l)
Demonstrate strong fiscal constraint in technology purchases	h
Demonstrate strong fiscal constraint in hiring procedures	h
Create and develop new and marketable services	m
Provide the systems to ensure timely, accurate reporting for decision-making purposes	h

Goal 4: Maximize Share Price Key Performance Factors	Significance (h/m/l)
Demonstrate strong fiscal constraint in technology purchases	m
Demonstrate strong fiscal constraint in hiring procedures	h
Create and develop new and marketable services	m
Provide the systems to ensure timely, accurate reporting for decision-making purposes	h

Goal 5: Maximize Market Share Key Performance Factors	Significance (h/m/l)
Create and develop new and marketable services	h
Ensure billing engines well maintained at all times	h
Provide accurate, timely market data	m
Build a strong allegiance with business management	h

Goal 6: Maximize Customer Satisfaction Key Performance Factors	Significance (h/m/l)
Ensure billing engines well maintained at all times	h
Provide accurate, timely customer data	m
Build a strong allegiance with business management	h

Goal 7: Reduce New Phone Activation Time Key Performance Factors	Significance (h/m/l)
Ensure activation gateway well maintained at all times	h
Reduce cycle time of activation process through waste analysis and reduction	m
Build a stronger allegiance with Customer Service	h

Goal 8: Minimize Churn Rate Key Performance Factors	Significance (h/m/l)
Ensure billing engines well maintained at all times	h
Provide accurate, timely customer data	m
Build a strong allegiance with business management	h

Goal 12: Maximize Billing Accuracy Key Performance Factors	Significance (h/m/l)
Ensure billing engines well maintained at all times	h
Do periodic inspections to ensure billing accuracy	m
Act on any billing problems immediately	h

Goal 15: Increase New Billable Service Revenue Key Performance Factors	Significance (h/m/l)
Create and develop new and marketable services	h
Build a strong allegiance with business management	h

ep 4: Organizing the KPFs into One List

Now that KPFs have been identified for all pertinent goals, it is time to organize the KPFs into one list, eliminating any duplicates that exist. Table 4-3 provides such a list for the IT department. Note that when duplicate KPFs are eliminated, the list shortens considerably.

Table 4-3 *IT KPF Summary*
Demonstrate strong fiscal constraint in technology purchases
Demonstrate strong fiscal constraint in hiring procedures
Create and develop new and marketable services
Provide the systems to ensure timely, accurate reporting for decision-making purposes
Ensure billing engines well maintained at all times
Provide accurate, timely market data
Provide accurate, timely customer data
Build a strong allegiance with business management
Do periodic inspections to ensure billing accuracy
Ensure activation gateway well maintained at all times
Reduce cycle time of activation process through waste analysis and reduction
Build a stronger allegiance with Customer Service
Act on any billing problems immediately

Step 5: Re-phrasing the KPFs into Departmental Goals

At this point, some of the KPFs are stated in general terms, and should be re-phrased into more goal-oriented terminology. By rephrasing them using goal-oriented terminology, they become ready for entry into the balanced scorecard. Table 4-4 shows the KPFs re-phrased into more goal-oriented terms. Sometimes one goal can be created that covers more than one KPF. An example of this is the goal "Minimize billing system downtime", which covers two KPFs (see Table 4-4).

Table 4-4
KPF — Goal Comparison

KPF	Goal
Demonstrate strong fiscal constraint in technology purchases	Minimize spending on technology, while maintaining system integrity
Demonstrate strong fiscal constraint in hiring procedures	Minimize number of new hires, while maintaining system integrity
Create and develop new and marketable services	Maximize the number of marketable services developed
Provide the systems to ensure timely, accurate reporting for decision-making purposes	Maximize systems usefulness for reporting purposes
Ensure billing engines well maintained at all times	Minimize billing system downtime (same as directly below)
Act on any billing problems immediately	Minimize billing system downtime (same as directly above)
Provide accurate, timely market data	Provide accurate, timely market data
Provide accurate, timely customer data	Provide accurate, timely customer data
Build a strong allegiance with business management	Optimize business management affiliations
Do periodic inspections to ensure billing accuracy	Optimize billing engine inspection frequency
Ensure activation gateway well maintained at all times	Minimize activation gateway downtime
Reduce cycle time of activation process through waste analysis and reduction	Minimize activation process cycle time
Build a stronger allegiance with Customer Service Department	Optimize Customer Service Department affiliation

ep 6: Categorizing the Departmental Goals

Now it is time to categorize each goal into one of the four balanced scorecard perspectives: financial; customer; internal business; and innovation and learning. Categorization techniques were discussed in Chapter 3. As was also mentioned in Chapter 3, the final decision regarding which perspective a goal falls under is not as crucial as maintaining momentum. The choice of perspective should not become an obstacle to moving forward, given the amount of work still to be done. Once goals have been categorized, a preliminary balanced scorecard summary can be established. Figure 4-6 provides a preliminary balanced scorecard summary for the IT Department.

Figure 4-6

Delphis Mobility
IT Department
Partial Balanced Scorecard Summary
2002

Financial Perspective			*Customer Perspective*		
Goals	**Measures**		**Goals**	**Measures**	
Minimize spending on technology, while maintaining system integrity			Provide accurate, timely market data		
Minimize number of new hires, while maintaining system integrity			Provide accurate, timely customer data		
			Optimize business management affiliations		
			Optimize Customer Service affiliation		
Internal Business Perspective			*Innovation & Learning Perspective*		
Goals	**Measures**		**Goals**	**Measures**	
Maximize system usefulness for reporting purposes			Maximize number of marketable services developed		
Minimize billing system downtime					
Optimize billing engine inspection frequency					
Minimize activation gateway downtime					
Minimize activation process cycle time					

Step 7: Adding Other Goals

At this point it is very unlikely that the departmental scorecard will be balanced and complete. This is due largely to the fact that, to this point, the scorecard has focused only on organizational-level goals. Each department will have its own set of goals, such as training and employee satisfaction, that need to be included. When adding goals, the four to seven goals per perspective guideline should be followed in order to seek balance. Typical departmental goals that will be added in at this point relate to:

- Departmental training, skills development;

- Department employee satisfaction, morale;

- Internal customer satisfaction (i.e., how pleased other departments within the organization are); and

- Departmental process improvements.

Something very important to consider here is that, any goals added in at this step should still somehow assist in achieving the overall organization strategy. If it does not, consideration should be given to why it has been included. For example, employee satisfaction is crucial to effective strategy deployment and therefore requires emphasis in each department. Even though HR was held accountable for overall employee satisfaction, each department should include this as a goal on their balanced scorecard.

Figure 4-7 provides an IT scorecard summary that includes some new goals. These additional goals reflect some initiatives that IT had been planning, as well as some that assist in satisfying the four to seven goals per perspective guideline. When goals have been added and the balance guideline has been met, the goals portion of Phase 2 is complete.

Figure 4-7

Delphis Mobility
IT Department
Partial Balanced Scorecard Summary
2002

Financial Perspective		Customer Perspective	
Goals	Measures	Goals	Measures
Minimize spending on technology, while maintaining system integrity		Provide accurate, timely market data	
Minimize number of new hires, while maintaining system integrity		Provide accurate, timely customer data	
Minimize discretionary IT expenditures		Optimize business management affiliations	
Maximize savings through activity analysis and waste reduction		Optimize Customer Service affiliation	
		Maximize satisfaction level of internal customer departments	
Internal Business Perspective		**Innovation & Learning Perspective**	
Goals	Measures	Goals	Measures
Maximize system usefulness for reporting purposes		Maximize number of marketable services developed	
Minimize billing system downtime		Maximize employee satisfaction ratio	
Optimize billing engine inspection frequency		Further enhance/develop IT-related skills as necessary	
Minimize activation gateway downtime		Assist HR with meeting certified project	
Minimize activation process cycle time			
Reduce cycle time of departmental project approval process			

☞ **An ideal stage at which to engage employees in the balanced scorecard process may be in the addition of goals. Soliciting employee input on additional goals can be beneficial in several ways. First, it provides an opportunity to introduce and educate employees on the scorecard implementation. Second, employees may have some excellent insight regarding goals that will assist in making the scorecard more balanced and complete. And finally, it promotes employee buy-in since their input will be reflected in the scorecard.**

Step 8: Determining Measures

Just like the organizational scorecard, measures must be assigned to each department scorecard goal so scores can be assigned later. The principles for department measures are consistent with those at the organization level. If necessary, please refer back to Chapter 3 regarding the measure determination procedure. Note once again that measures can take many forms: percentages; dollars; number of days; etc. It must be made very clear what the unit(s) of measure will be, so that there are no misunderstandings or miscommunications later in the process.

Defining Measures

As was mentioned in Chapter 3, it is extremely important to define measures in such a way that they will not be disputed at a later time, thus compromising the long-term success of the scorecard implementation. By providing clear guidelines and definitions around what a measure consists of, different interpretations and unnecessary conflict can be avoided during the scoring period. A great example of a measure that can take many meanings is "on-time delivery". How is on-time delivery defined? Is it defined by the organization, or by the customer? What if one customer defines on-time delivery as anything within three days, and another anything within three weeks? Some strict parameters need to be set around measure definitions. It may seem like a step that could be glossed over in the initial stages, but is actually very important.

Figure 4-8 provides a scorecard summary for IT that includes a measure for each goal.

Figure 4-8

Delphis Mobility
IT Department
Balanced Scorecard Summary
2002

Financial Perspective			*Customer Perspective*	
Goals	**Measures**		**Goals**	**Measures**
Minimize spending on technology, while maintaining system integrity	Actual dollar spend (vs. benchmark, in $M)		Provide accurate, timely market data	Actual accuracy, timeliness of market data
Minimize number of new hires, while maintaining system integrity	Actual number of hires (vs. benchmark)		Provide accurate, timely customer data	Actual accuracy, timeliness of customer data
Minimize discretionary IT expenditures	Actual dollar spend (vs. benchmark, in $M)		Optimize business management affiliations	Actual internal customer survey results
Maximize savings through activity analysis and waste reduction	Total demonstrated savings (in $M)		Optimize Customer Service Department affiliation	Actual internal customer survey results
			Maximize satisfaction level of internal customer departments	Actual internal customer survey results
Internal Business Perspective			*Innovation & Learning Perspective*	
Goals	**Measures**		**Goals**	**Measures**
Maximize system usefulness for reporting purposes	Actual satisfaction survey results		Maximize number of marketable services developed	Actual number of marketable services developed
Minimize billing system downtime	Actual total hours of downtime		Maximize employee satisfaction index	Actual employee satisfaction index
Optimize billing engine inspection frequency	Total number of inspections		Further enhance/develop IT-related skills as necessary	Total average number of approved training days per employee
Minimize activation gateway downtime	Actual total hours of downtime		Assist HR with meeting certified project manager targets	Number of certified project managers in IT
Minimize activation process cycle time	Average actual cycle time on November 30, 2002			
Reduce cycle time of departmental project approval process	Actual average cycle time (days)			

›p 9: Assigning Weights

Again, like the organizational scorecard, assigning weights is necessary to prioritize the many scorecard components. Since the weight-assigning rationale and procedure is identical to that of the organizational scorecard, please refer back to Chapter 3 regarding the weight assigning procedure. It is important to note again that there are actually two weighting exercises that must take place. The first is the weighting by scorecard perspective.

Figure 4-9 provides a summary for the IT balanced scorecard that includes weighting for each perspective. The second weighting exercise is for the goals within each perspective. Figures 4-10 to 4-13 provide a possible weighting scenario for all goals for each of the perspectives: financial (Figure 4-10); customer (Figure 4-11); internal business process (Figure 4-12); and innovation and learning (Figure 4-13). It is useful to refer back to the "Significance" column set up on the KPF summary documentation; this plus the frequency that each goal appeared as a KPF should assist in assigning weights.

Figure 4-9

Delphis Mobility
IT Department
Balanced Scorecard Weighting Summary
2002

	Weighting
Financial Perspective	20%
Customer Perspective	35%
Internal Business Perspective	25%
Innovation & Learning Perspective	20%
Total Weighting (must = 100%)	100%

Figure 4-10

Delphis Mobility
IT Department
Financial Perspective
2002

Goals	Weight	Measures
Minimize spending on technology, while maintaining system integrity	35%	Actual dollar spend (vs. benchmark, in $M)
Minimize number of new hires, while maintaining system integrity	30%	Actual number of hires (vs. benchmark)
Minimize discretionary IT expenditures	20%	Actual dollar spend (vs. benchmark, in $M)
Maximize savings through activity analysis and waste reduction	15%	Total demonstrated savings
Total Weight (must = 100%)	100%	

Figure 4-11

Delphis Mobility
IT Department
Customer Perspective
2002

Goals	Weight	Measures
Provide accurate, timely market data	20%	Actual accuracy, timeliness of market data
Provide accurate, timely customer data	20%	Actual accuracy, timeliness of customer data
Optimize business management affiliations	20%	Actual internal customer survey results
Optimize Customer Service Department affiliation	15%	Actual internal customer survey results
Maximize satisfaction level of internal customer departments	25%	Actual internal customer survey results
Total Weight (must = 100%)	**100%**	

* score range is from -2 to +2

Figure 4-12

Delphis Mobility
IT Department
Internal Business Perspective
2002

Goals	Weight	Measures
Maximize system usefulness for reporting purposes	20%	Actual satisfaction survey results
Minimize billing system downtime	15%	Actual total hours of downtime
Optimize billing engine inspection frequency	10%	Total number of inspections
Minimize activation gateway downtime	20%	Actual total hours of downtime
Minimize activation process cycle time	20%	Average actual cycle time on November 30, 2002
Reduce cycle time of departmental project approval process	15%	Actual average cycle time (days)
Total Weight (must = 100%)	**100%**	

Figure 4-13

Delphis Mobility
IT Department
Innovation & Learning Perspective
2002

Goals	Weight	Measures
Maximize number of marketable services developed	30%	Actual number of marketable services developed
Maximize employee satisfaction index	35%	Actual employee satisfaction index
Further enhance/develop IT-related skills as necessary	20%	Total average number of approved training days per employee
Assist HR with meeting certified project manager targets	15%	Number of certified project managers in IT
Total Weight (must = 100%)	**100%**	

10: Setting Targets and Stretch Goals

Setting targets is necessary so that at the end of the performance period, actual results can be compared to targets and performance assessed. Since the target-setting procedure is identical to that of the organizational scorecard, please refer back to Chapter 3 regarding the target setting procedure. Note once again that target and stretch goals should be stated in the same form as the stated measure for the goal in question (i.e., percentages, dollars, etc.). Figures 4-14 to 4-17 provide target and stretch goals for each of the perspectives: financial (Figure 4-14); customer (Figure 4-15); internal business process (Figure 4-16); and innovation and learning (Figure 4-17).

Figure 4-14

Delphis Mobility
IT Department
Financial Perspective
2002

Goals	Weight	Measures	Target	Stretch
Minimize spending on technology, while maintaining system integrity	35%	Actual dollar spend (vs. benchmark, in $M)	$ 40	$ 38
Minimize number of new hires, while maintaining system integrity	30%	Actual number of hires (vs. benchmark)	20	15
Minimize discretionary IT expenditures	20%	Actual dollar spend (vs. benchmark, in $M)	$ 5	$ 4
Maximize savings through activity analysis and waste reduction	15%	Total demonstrated savings	$ 3	$ 4
Total Weight (must = 100%)	**100%**			

Figure 4-15

Delphis Mobility
IT Department
Customer Perspective
2002

Goals	Weight	Measures	Target	Stretch
Provide accurate, timely market data	20%	Actual accuracy, timeliness of market data	97%	99%
Provide accurate, timely customer data	20%	Actual accuracy, timeliness of customer data	98%	99%
Optimize business management affiliations	20%	Actual internal customer survey results	80%	90%
Optimize Customer Service Department affiliation	15%	Actual internal customer survey results	85%	90%
Maximize satisfaction level of internal customer departments	25%	Actual internal customer survey results	85%	88%
Total Weight (must = 100%)	**100%**			

Figure 4-16

Delphis Mobility
IT Department
Internal Business Perspective
2002

Goals	Weight	Measures	Target	Stretch
Maximize system usefulness for reporting purposes	20%	Actual satisfaction survey results	85%	95%
Minimize billing system downtime	15%	Actual total hours of downtime	100	80
Optimize billing engine inspection frequency	10%	Total number of inspections	24	26
Minimize activation gateway downtime	20%	Actual total hours of downtime	75	60
Minimize activation process cycle time	20%	Average actual cycle time on November 30, 2002	13	11
Reduce cycle time of departmental project approval process	15%	Actual average cycle time (days)	1.5	1.0

Total Weight (must = 100%)   **100%**

Figure 4-17

Delphis Mobility
IT Department
Innovation & Learning Perspective
2002

Goals	Weight	Measures	Target	Stretch
Maximize number of marketable services developed	30%	Actual number of marketable services developed	2	4
Maximize employee satisfaction index	35%	Actual employee satisfaction index	80%	90%
Further enhance/develop IT-related skills as necessary	20%	Total average number of approved training days per employee	4	5
Assist HR with meeting certified project manager targets	15%	Number of certified project managers in IT	30	35

Total Weight (must = 100%)   **100%**

Step 11: Reviewing for Balance and Completeness

At this point the first draft of the departmental scorecard (or scorecards) are complete. However, it is not truly complete until several knowledgeable people have reviewed it for appropriateness, balance, and completeness. The model used to construct the scorecard is by necessity somewhat generic and as such each resulting scorecard should be reviewed, revised and enhanced where necessary so that it is the most ideal scorecard possible. In order to maximize the likelihood of acceptance, it must have the right look and feel for those actually in the department.

Summary

At this point the departmental scorecard phase is complete. The process is not, however. It is very important at this point to communicate the scorecard through the department. There should also be some mechanism for employees to ask questions and voice concerns. Effective change management, discussed later in the book, is crucial to the success of the scorecard initiative. It is strongly recommended that change management techniques be employed wherever applicable.

While the departmental balanced scorecard is a major accomplishment, it is unfortunately not always enough. The fact is, even the department scorecard may not be ideally suited as a performance measurement tool for most departmental employees. They simply may not be able to relate to some or most of the scorecard. The next crucial step is to cascade the scorecard down one more level to the most important aspect of any organization: the employees. This is the subject of the next chapter.

☞ **The cascade process described in this chapter has assumed that the organization is composed of a series of departments only (i.e., there are no divisions or sub-units). If an organization is structured such that there are divisions or operating sub-units, the cascade principles in the chapter do not change. What does change is that the number of cascade phases will increase. For example, an organization with divisions will first cascade the organization scorecard down to the divisions, then to the departments within the division. The process is identical, just done twice instead of once to reach the department level.**

Chapter 5

The Employee-Level Cascade

Overview

With the department-level scorecards complete, it is now appropriate to begin the process of cascading the scorecard to the appropriate employees of each department. Before embarking on this phase, it is necessary to review why the process of cascading to the individual level is so important.

The Importance of the Employee-Level Cascade

Just to review, it was reasoned in Chapter 4 that the organization-level scorecard is not ideally suited as a performance measurement tool for most departmental employees. Departmental scorecards assist greatly in making a stronger connection between employees and strategy, and provide a tool that is much more relatable. Still, the connection between strategy and specific employee action is often not totally apparent from the departmental scorecard. To make that connection clear and understandable to employees, an individual scorecard is far superior the others. Done properly, the individual scorecard lays out clear expectations for employees regarding performance measurement and evaluation.

Important Considerations of Phase 3

Some important considerations in performing the employee cascade process are:

1. Who should actually perform the work of completing these steps?

2. How long should Phase 3 take?

3. What if we hit a roadblock?

4. Which employees should have an individual scorecard?

Each of these concerns is addressed below.

Work Performance

It is highly recommended that a cross-functional team within the department be dedicated to this phase, at least for Step 1. Ideally, someone from each functional area within the department would be on this team, so that representation and input from all parties in the department is ensured. It is appropriate to include internal customers wherever possible also. For example, for the goal "Maximize satisfaction of internal customer departments", the input of those internal customer departments is necessary in order to thoroughly analyze this goal. Again, an external facilitator is recommended at various times throughout the project, especially at the outset of the cascade process. The start of the exercise generally dictates the longer-term success or failure — a good start is vital.

If for some reason the team is not fully cross-functional, it is important that individuals from each area within the department not represented be kept "in the loop", and allowed to have input on a less formal basis. The major consequence of not including all areas involved is the serious risk of a lack of ownership and buy-in by those areas that feel "out of the loop". Another consequence is the fact that, for each area not represented; there is a loss of valuable input from that area of expertise. Stated simply, the model cannot be considered complete unless representation from all areas has been included. It is crucial to include all areas on the team.

A very important consideration is that those appointed to the scorecard team need to be able to dedicate a significant amount of their time to the scorecard project, ideally on a full-time basis. It simply cannot be an "after-hours" project. If so, it is doomed to fail. There needs to be resource planning so that team members are not working on the scorecard project as well as all of their regular duties.

Once steps one to three are complete, it is possible for each manager to assume responsibility for the scorecards of their own employees. Another option is to keep the team in charge throughout the entire cascade process. The specific organizational circumstances should dictate which is most appropriate. No matter what approach is taken, it is imperative to have a project owner within the department who is responsible for monitoring departmental progress and taking action where necessary. If just one manager falls behind, the entire project could be delayed. It is crucial to have someone stay on top of this.

ation

The total period of time for the implementation of Phase 3 can range anywhere from three months to one year, depending on several things, such as the number of areas in the department, number of scorecard goals, number of dedicated staff, and so on. Figure 5-1 provides a possible Phase 3 timeline, indicating how long each step in Phase 3 can take. These are estimates that can be used as a general guideline.

Figure 5-1

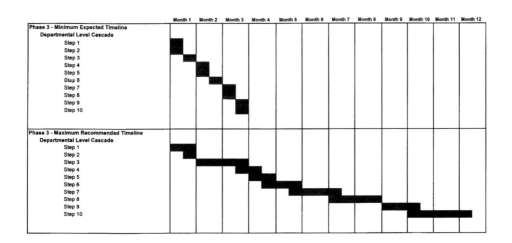

Encountering Roadblocks

Roadblocks are an unfortunate but inevitable part of any major initiative. Some typical roadblocks that will be encountered during this phase are:

- Determining which employees should have an individual scorecard;

- Determining the materiality of an employee's impact;

- Determining the complete set of KPFs;

- Defining measures for each goal;

- Agreeing on the appropriate weights; and

- Agreeing on targets and stretch goals.

If roadblocks are encountered, it may be advisable to assign a facilitator to mediate. This could be someone from a higher level in the organization, or an outside expert in the field. The important thing to keep in mind is that balanced scorecard implementation is a long process — minor roadblocks should not be allowed to become the causes of major delay.

Determining Which Employees to Cascade

In Phase 2, cascading to every department was recommended for several reasons. In Phase 3, however, it is not recommended that each and every employee throughout the organization have an individual scorecard. At some point, or at some level, diminishing returns will be realized to the point where the benefits of an individual scorecard for certain employees will not be worth the additional costs incurred to create and maintain it. The issue then becomes where this line should be drawn — an issue that has no ready solution. Chapter 7 will discuss strategies for determining the most appropriate cut-off.

Phase 3: The Step-by-Step View

The major initiative of this phase of the cascading process is to create a balanced scorecard for each employee considered to have a role significant enough to merit the effort and involvement necessary to maintain an individual scorecard. The departmental scorecard is used as the blueprint or guide. This is a significant undertaking, and is best achieved by breaking the phase down into the following steps:

1. For each goal, determine the employee(s) that have a material impact;

2. Re-organize the results from the first step into employee summaries;

3. For those employees identified, determine what the specific impact(s) on the goal are (referred to as key performance factors, or KPFs);

4. Organize the KPFs into one list, eliminating duplicates;

5. Re-phrase the KPFs into employee goals;

6. Add any other appropriate goals;

7. Determine how each goal will be measured;

8. Assign weights to each perspective, and each goal;

9. Set targets and stretch goals; and

10. Review for balance and completeness.

Figure 5-2 provides a pictorial view of the entire process. It is worth noting that the individual cascade process is virtually identical to the departmental cascade process except for one large exception. Step 6 in Phase 2 was to organize the goals into the four balanced scorecard perspectives. In this phase, there is no need to do this since the individual scorecard does not need to be broken out by perspective.

Figure 5-2
Phase 3 Overview

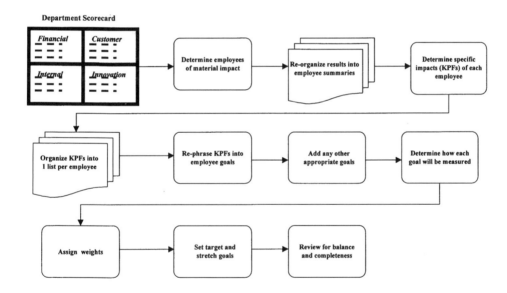

Step 1: Determining the Employees of Material Impact

At this point, the departmental scorecard is reviewed, goal by goal, to determine the employees that have a material impact on each goal. As discussed in the previous chapter, the term "material" can have many interpretations; it should be considered to mean that the impact of the employee on the goal in question must be significant enough to be worth the additional administrative work required to track and measure it on a scorecard. This is a judgement call. If unsure whether a employee's impact is material, or there is debate about it, it is advisable to include it as material. If at a later time it is deemed immaterial, or the employee's scorecard becomes too complex, it can be eliminated.

During this step, it is not imperative to identify exactly how an employee impacts a departmental goal. In fact, this level of detail is discouraged, since it can slow the progress of this step. Instead, the main objective should be to identify all employees having a material impact. Often this will be very obvious. For example, for the goal of minimizing new hires, it is pretty obvious that those involved in departmental hiring decisions have a large impact. Similarly, for the goal of minimizing discretionary expenditures, the contribution of the hiring decision-makers is fairly evident. Sometimes the impact is less obvious, and some thought needs to go into determining whether the employee has material impact. Any notes taken when determining whether an employee does have a material impact should be kept for the next stage. Due to the fact that there will be many goals to go through, and many employees to identify, it is advisable to keep the analysis at a high level during this step, saving the detailed analysis for subsequent steps.

Figure 5-3 re-creates the illustrated view of the "fishbone" method to record all the employees deemed to have a material impact on each department goal. In this view, the department scorecard goal is put at the front arrow, and all employees having a material impact are listed. Many people find that the pictorial view is useful in keeping clear which employees impact which goals. This process continues for each scorecard goal until all employees having material impact have been identified. This step can be considered complete when each department goal has had an impact analysis done. Once complete, there will be a "fishbone" for each department goal, just like in Phase 2. Table 5-1 summarizes the employees impacting each goal for IT Department after the impact determination has been performed on all goals in the IT Department's scorecard.

Figure 5-3
Delphis Mobility
Departmental Impact Analysis — Pictorial View

Goal: Reduce Cycle Time of Project Approval Process

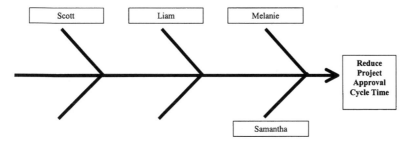

Goal: Further Enhance/Develop Skills As Necessary

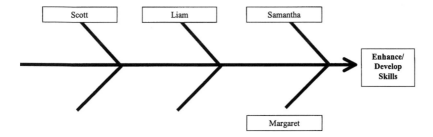

Table 5-1

Department Goal/Employee Impact Summary	
Department Goals	Employees of Impact
1. Minimize technology spend	Margaret, Griffin, Scott
2. Minimize number of new hires	Scott, Liam, Samantha, Margaret
3. Minimize discretionary expenditures	Scott, Liam, Margaret
4. Maximize savings through activity analysis and waste reduction	Scott, Melanie, Karen
5. Provide accurate, timely market data	Tim, Liam
6. Provide accurate, timely customer data	Tim, Liam
7. Optimize business management affiliations	Liam, Nancy, Samantha, Tim, Joe
8. Optimize Customer Service Department affiliations	Liam, Nancy, Tim, Joe
9. Maximize satisfaction of internal customer departments	Scott, Liam, Samantha, Margaret
10. Maximize system usefulness for reporting purposes	Scott, Melanie, Griffin
11. Minimize billing engine downtime	Margaret, Griffin, Kelsey
12. Optimize billing engine inspection frequency	Margaret, Griffin, Kelsey
13. Minimize activation gateway downtime	Leanne, Corinne, Karen
14. Minimize activation process cycle time	Leanne, Corinne, Karen
15. Reduce cycle time of departmental project approval process	Scott, Liam, Samantha, Melanie
16. Maximize number of marketable services developed	Scott, Samantha, Melanie
17. Maximize employee satisfaction index	Scott, Liam, Samantha, Margaret
18. Further enhance/develop skills as necessary	Scott, Liam, Samantha, Margaret, Nancy
19. Assist HR with meeting certified project manager targets	Scott, Liam, Samantha, Margaret, Nancy

p 2: Reorganization of Analysis Results into Employee Summaries

At this point, there are a number of departmental goals and employees involved in the analysis. It is possible to reorganize the information by splitting off the employees from one another, and forming a summary for each employee. Figure 5-4 provides a graphical representation of this reorganization process. Table 5-2 provides a summary for the Director of Strategic Projects, Samantha. In an actual implementation, this would be done for all employees who will be measured using the individual balanced scorecard. Samantha will be the example employee throughout this chapter, so only she will be followed here forward. Please see the section "Samantha's Profile" on the next page for a brief description of Samantha's role in the IT Department at Delphis Mobility.

Figure 5-4
Reorganizing KPF Results

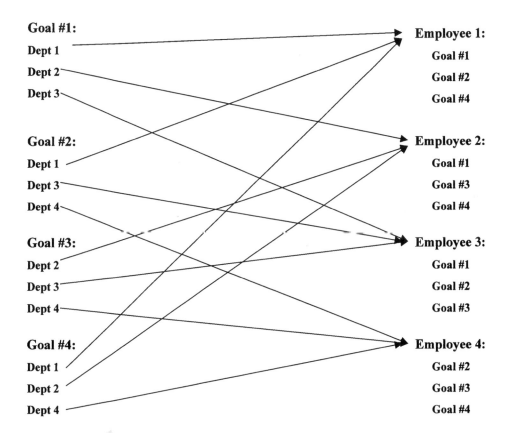

Samantha's Profile

Samantha has been the Business Integration Director of the IT Department for the past three years, and has 47 staff reporting directly to her. Her key position tasks include:

- Working with other departments in the company to determine how IT can best suit the needs of the rest of the organization;

- Prioritizing and reviewing the lengthy list of project proposals;

- Approving projects;

- Hiring business integration managers (and sometimes analysts); and

- Meeting regularly with other departments regarding project status.

Table 5-2

Samantha's Departmental Goal Impact Summary
2.   Minimize number of new hires
7.   Optimize business management affiliations
9.   Maximize satisfaction of internal customer departments
15. Reduce cycle time of departmental project approval process
16. Maximize number of marketable services developed
17. Maximize employee satisfaction index
18. Further enhance/develop skills as necessary
19. Assist HR with meeting certified project manager targets

Step 3: Key Performance Factor Analysis

Now that each employee has been neatly organized around the specific goals they impact, the next step is to perform a more detailed analysis on each employee about how they specifically impact the goal(s) identified. In performing this analysis exercise, the main question that needs to be asked for each goal identified is, "For this goal, what does this employee need to do to assist in achieving the goal?" As in Chapter 4, the answer (or answers) to this question can be referred to as a key performance factor, or KPF. KPFs can be defined as those actions that will assist the organization in achieving its stated goal(s), and are stated as an action. For example, an employee KPF for the goal of profit maximization could be "to demonstrate strong fiscal constraint in technology purchases".

A couple more points on the merit of KPFs. First, there can, and often will, be more than one KPF for a given goal. It is important to identify all KPFs related to a goal — otherwise, the risk of an incomplete scorecard increases. Second, generally speaking, the lower down in the organization the cascading process goes, the more specific the KPFs will become. This is consistent with the migration from strategic and functional objectives toward more operational objectives. The KPFs identified in this chapter will be noticeably more specific than the department KPFs identified in Phase 2.

This KPF exercise, just like the first one, requires a great amount of brainstorming. It should include the input of knowledgeable people across several areas of the department, even outside the department where appropriate. For Samantha, a brainstorming session should result in a list of items like that found in Figure 5-5, which is called an Employee KPF Summary Document. Note that in Figure 5-5, several of the KPFs are found to apply to more than one goal. For example, the KPF "Complete project proposal documentation completely and accurately" is identified for several goals, including:

- Maximize satisfaction of internal customer departments;

- Reduce cycle time of departmental project approval process; and

- Maximize savings through activity analysis and waste reduction.

Note that, just like in Phase 2, there is a column to the far right entitled "Significance". It is recommended that this column be used to indicate the degree of significance of the KPF on the goal: high, medium, or low. This will help later when assigning weights. Generally speaking, the lower the level of significance, the smaller the weight of the KPF. Note that the degree of significance of a KPF can be different, depending on the goal. For example, the KPF "Complete project proposal documentation completely and accurately" was given a medium rating for the goal "Maximize savings through activity analysis and waste reduction", given the relatively minor contribution it makes toward overall savings. However, the same KPF was given a high rating for the goal "Maximize satisfaction of internal customer departments", since it has a much higher impact on this goal. It is appropriate to have different ratings for different goals, and having this information will help in the weighting exercise.

Figure 5-5

Delphis Mobility — IT Department Balanced Scorecard Employee KPF Summary	
Employee: Samantha *Goal 2: Minimize Number of New Hires*	
Key Performance Factors	Significance (h/m/l)
Demonstrate strong fiscal constraint in hiring procedures	h
Prioritize workload effectively	m
Goal 7: Optimize Business Management Affiliations Key Performance Factors	Significance (h/m/l)
Assist Marketing Department with strategic endeavors as necessary	h
Work with Network Department to identify and satisfy needs as appropriate	h
Goal 9: Maximize Satisfaction of Internal Customer Departments Key Performance Factors	Significance (h/m/l)
Complete project proposal documentation completely and accurately	h
Assist Marketing Department with strategic endeavors as necessary	m
Work with Network Department to identify and satisfy needs as appropriate	m
Act on project proposals waiting for sign-off within 24 hours	m
Ensure all staff attend the company's "internal customer service" course offering by December 31st	h
Provide information to various departments as requested accurately and on a timely basis	m
Prioritize workload effectively	m

Figure 5-5 cont *Delphis Mobility — IT Department* *Balanced Scorecard* *Employee KPF Summary*	
Employee: Samantha	
Goal 15: Reduce Cycle Time of Departmental Project Approval Process Key Performance Factors	Significance (h/m/l)
Complete project proposal documentation completely and accurately	H
Act on project proposals waiting for sign-off within 24 hours	H
Goal 16: Maximize Number of Marketable Services Developed Key Performance Factors	Significance (h/m/l)
Assist Marketing Department with strategic endeavors as necessary	H
Goal 17: Maximize Employee Satisfaction Index Key Performance Factors	Significance (h/m/l)
Work with employees to improve employee satisfaction	H
Employee: Samantha *Goal 18: Further Enhance/Develop Skills as Necessary* Key Performance Factors	Significance (h/m/l)
Increase number of staff certified in project management	h
Ensure all staff attend the company's "internal customer service" course offering by December 31st	h
Goal 19: Assist HR With Meeting Certified Project Manager Targets Key Performance Factors	Significance (h/m/l)
Increase number of staff certified in project management	h

Step 4: Organizing the KPFs into One List

Now that KPFs have been identified for all goals relevant to Samantha, it is time to organize the KPFs into one list, eliminating any duplicates that exist. Table 5-3 provides such a list for Samantha. Note that when duplicate KPFs are eliminated, the list shortens considerably.

Table 5-3

Samantha's KPF List
Demonstrate strong fiscal constraint in hiring procedures
Prioritize workload effectively
Complete project proposal documentation completely and accurately
Assist Marketing Department with strategic endeavors as necessary
Work with Network Department to identify and satisfy needs as appropriate
Ensure all staff attend the company's "internal customer service" course offering by December 31st
Act on project proposals waiting for sign-off within 24 hours
Provide information to various departments as requested accurately and on a timely basis
Work with employees to improve employee satisfaction
Increase number of staff certified in project management

Step 5: Re-phrasing the KPFs into Departmental Goals

At this point, some of the KPFs are stated in general terms, and need to be re-phrased into more goal-oriented terminology suitable for entry into the employee's balanced scorecard. In addition, often two or more KPFs can be combined into one goal. For example, two of Samantha's KPFs, "Assist Marketing Department with strategic endeavors as necessary" and "Work with Network Department to identify and satisfy needs as appropriate" are both internal customer-focused. It is appropriate in this case to combine these KPFs into one goal. Table 5-4 shows Samantha's KPFs re-phrased and, where appropriate, combined into one goal.

Another noteworthy observation is the fact that the goal "Maximize satisfaction of internal customer departments" was broken down into KPFs for Samantha, then combined once again into a single goal, "Maximize internal customer satisfaction index". This was done based on the assumption that the satisfaction index measure will cover each KPF area, therefore affording the ability to create fewer total goals. One of either the goal or measure(s) should cover the specific objectives of the employee KPFs. If the satisfaction index does not address the KPFs, then it may be wise to create separate goals for each KPF. The most important thing to keep in mind is that the specific methodology used to create the detailed elements of the scorecard should be what is best under the exact circumstances of the organization.

Table 5-4

KPF — Goal Comparison	
KPF	Goal
Demonstrate strong fiscal constraint in hiring procedures	Minimize number of new hires, while maintaining department integrity
Complete project proposal documentation completely and accurately	Maximize accuracy and timeliness of project proposal documentation (same as directly below)
Act on project proposals waiting for sign-off within 24 hours	Maximize accuracy and timeliness of project proposal documentation (same as directly above)
Assist Marketing Department with strategic endeavors as necessary	Maximize internal customer satisfaction index (same as directly below)
Work with Network Department to identify and satisfy needs as appropriate	Maximize internal customer satisfaction index (same as directly above and below)
Prioritize workload effectively	Maximize internal customer satisfaction index (same as directly above and below)
Provide information to various departments as requested accurately and on a timely basis	Maximize internal customer satisfaction index (same as directly above)
Ensure all staff attend the company's "internal customer service" course offering by December 31st	Increase/develop employee skills (same as directly below)
Increase number of staff certified in project management	Increase/develop employee skills (same as directly above)
Work with employees to improve employee satisfaction	Increase employee satisfaction index

p 6: Creating the Preliminary Scorecard

Now it is time to take the results of Steps 1 to 5 and place them into an individual scorecard template for further analysis. Unlike Phase 2, which categorized goals into one of four perspectives, it is not necessary to categorize employee scorecard goals into perspectives. There are three main reasons for this. First, if Phases 1 and 2 have been done correctly, the probability of balance existing in the employee scorecards is very high. Second, a large amount of time and effort are inherent in completing Phase 3. Coupling this with the high probability of balance just discussed, the benefits of taking the extra step of categorizing employee goals usually do not justify the additional time and effort. Finally, the final step in Phase 3 is to check for balance and completeness. During this step, any obvious imbalances that may have somehow crept in can be identified and dealt with.

Figure 5-6 provides a preliminary balanced scorecard for Samantha. At this point the scorecard is preliminary — there are several more steps to completion.

Figure 5-6

Partial Individual Balanced Scorecard
Delphis Mobility
IT Department
2002

Employee Name: | **Samantha**

Goals	Weight	Measures
Minimize number of new hires, while maintaining system integrity		
Maximize accuracy and timeliness of project proposal documentation		
Maximize internal customer satisfaction index		
Increase/develop employee skills		
Increase employee satisfaction index		

Step 7: Adding Other Goals

At this point it is unlikely that the employee scorecard will look complete. This is due largely to the fact that, to this point, the scorecard has focused only on departmental goals. A goal or goals specific to each employee may be appropriate and thus merit inclusion. In Samantha's case, she had agreed to head up a task force aimed at ensuring that the company spends enough on qualifying research and development to meet its licensing agreement. While this did not initially appear on Samantha's scorecard through the regular cascading process, it is significant and thus merits inclusion.

Something very important to consider here is that, any goal added in at this step should still somehow assist in achieving the overall organization strategy. If it does not, consideration should be given as to why it has been included. Going back to the research and development goal added for Samantha, if the company's license was ever suspended the whole strategy is jeopardized. This goal thus becomes very important to strategy in an indirect manner and therefore is included.

☞ **If an employee has not yet been involved in the scorecard process, an ideal stage to engage the employee in the process may be in the addition of goals. Soliciting employee input on additional goals can be beneficial in several ways. First, it provides an opportunity to introduce and educate employees on the scorecard implementation. Second, employees may have some excellent insight regarding goals that will assist in making their scorecard more balanced and complete. And finally, it promotes employee buy-in and ownership since their input will be reflected in the scorecard.**

It is recommended that three more specific goals always be added to any individual balanced scorecard. The first is a goal that seeks to maximize the individual's sense of teamwork and ability to work well with others. One danger in evaluating individuals based on a scorecard approach is the chance that some may work to maximize their scorecard results at any cost. It is clearly not in the organization's best interests if an employee is cutting corners, stepping on toes or refusing to assist others they should be helping just because it is not explicitly represented on their scorecard. Adding a goal that strives toward maximizing this element of the employee's "unwritten job description" is highly recommended. There are several possible names for this goal — "Service With a Smile" is one possibility (SWAS for short). Including a goal such as this sends the message that the scorecard is not a tool to be manipulated and maximized at any price. Failure by any employee to recognize this should ultimately lead to a low SWAS score, thus giving management the ability to correct (to some degree) for this type of behavior and send an appropriate message.

The next recommended additional goal is for the employee to strive toward maximizing the department's scorecard results. There is a danger, however small, that the individual scorecard approach to performance measurement may create an "every person for themselves" mentality. For many obvious reasons, this is not a desirable effect. While the SWAS goal discussed above can help avoid this problem to some degree, alone it is not enough. It is therefore recommended that each employee have a scorecard goal to assist in maximizing the department's scorecard score. This will help promote and reinforce the teamwork and unity that should exist with any performance measurement system. The balanced scorecard is a tool that can be used to create a team environment within the department — adding this goal can assist greatly with this.

The final recommended additional goal is for the employee to strive toward maximizing the organization's scorecard results. For reasons very similar to those discussed above regarding the departmental scorecard results, a similar goal at the organizational level is highly recommended. The balanced scorecard again is a tool that can be used to create a team environment throughout the entire organization — adding this goal can assist greatly with this.

Figure 5-7 provides a more comprehensive scorecard for Samantha, which includes all the additional goals discussed above.

Figure 5-7
Partial Individual Balanced Scorecard
Delphis Mobility
IT Department
2002

Employee Name:	Samantha

Goals	Weight	Measures
Minimize number of new hires, while maintaining system integrity		
Maximize accuracy and timeliness of project proposal documentation		
Maximize internal customer satisfaction index		
Increase/develop employee skills		
Increase/develop employee skills		
Increase employee satisfaction index		
Maximize dollar amount of research and development claim		
SWAS		
Maximize department scorecard score		
Maximize organizational scorecard score		

Step 8: Determining Measures

Just like the departmental scorecard, measures must be assigned to each employee scorecard goal so scores can be assigned later. The principles for employee measures are consistent with those at both the organization and departmental levels. If necessary please refer back to Chapter 3 regarding the measure determination procedure. Note once again that measures can take many forms: percentages, dollars, number of days, etc. It must be made very clear what the unit(s) of measure will be, so that there are no misunderstandings or miscommunications later in the process.

Defining Measures

As was mentioned in Chapters 3 and 4, it is extremely important to define measures in a way that they will not be disputed at a later time, thus risking the long-term success of the scorecard implementation. By providing clear guidelines and definitions around what a measure consists of, different interpretations and unnecessary conflict during the scoring period can be avoided. A great example of a measure that can take many meanings is "on-time delivery". How is on-time delivery defined? Is it defined by the organization, or by the customer? What if one customer defines on-time delivery as anything within three days, and another anything within three weeks? Some strict parameters need to be set around measure definitions. It may seem like a step that could be glossed over in the initial stages, but is actually very important.

An important consideration with the individual scorecard is the fact that there are usually some subjective goals set. For example, a goal often used for an employee would be how well they treat other employees and peers (e.g., the SWAS goal used in for Samantha). Clearly there is very little or no objective data to use as measures for these types of goals. Use of these subjective goals is perfectly fine. For subjective goals, the "measures" section should describe the type of subjective criteria that will be used. Instead of providing stretch and target goals, the term "Subjective Score" should be used on the scorecard where target and stretch goals are normally entered. The scoring of subjective goals will be discussed in the next chapter.

ep 9: Assigning Weights

Like the organizational and departmental scorecards, assigning weights is necessary to prioritize the many scorecard components. The weight-assigning rationale and procedure is somewhat simpler for the employee scorecard compared to that of the organizational and departmental scorecards. Since there are no perspectives in the individual scorecard, only a goal-weighting procedure need take place.

> ☞ **Another ideal place to actively solicit employee input is in the weighting of the scorecard. Allowing an employee to have a voice in the weighting of their scorecard makes sense and can be beneficial in several ways. First, it provides an opportunity and challenges the employee to really think through and understand the scorecard implementation. Second, employees may have some excellent insight regarding the appropriate weights that will assist in making their scorecard more accurate and reflective of their role. And finally, it promotes employee buy-in and ownership, since their input will be reflected in the scorecard.**

ep 10: Setting Targets and Stretch Goals

Setting targets is necessary so that at the end of the performance period, actual results can be compared to targets and performance assessed. Since the target-setting procedure is identical to that of the organization scorecard, please refer back to Chapter 3 regarding the target-setting procedure. Note once again that target and stretch goals should be started in the same form as the stated measure for the goal in question (i.e., percentages, dollars, etc.).

ep 11: Reviewing for Balance and Completeness

At this point the first draft of a finished individual scorecard (or scorecards) is complete. However, it is not truly complete until several knowledgeable people have reviewed it for appropriateness, balance, and completeness. The model used to construct the scorecard is by necessity somewhat generic and as such each resulting scorecard needs to be reviewed and revised and enhanced where necessary so that it is the most ideal scorecard possible. In order to maximize the likelihood of acceptance, it must have the right look and feel for the employee and where appropriate others in the department. It should also be consistent with all the other scorecards in the department and across the organization.

Figure 5-8 provides a completed scorecard for Samantha, which one can assume has been approved by all parties involved.

Figure 5-8

Individual Balanced Scorecard
Delphis Mobility
IT Department
2002

Employee Name: Samantha

Goals	Weight	Measures	Target	Stretch
Minimize number of new hires, while maintaining system integrity	10%	Actual number of new hires	10	8
Maximize accuracy and timeliness of project proposal documentation	10%	Percentage of project proposals submitted accurately and on time	90%	95%
Maximize internal customer satisfaction index	20%	Actual internal customer satisfaction index score	90%	95%
Increase/develop employee skills	5%	Percentage of employees that obtain project management or other approved certification	95%	98%
Increase/develop employee skills	5%	Percentage of employees that attend company's 'internal customer service' course	95%	100%
Increase employee satisfaction index	15%	Actual employee satisfaction index score	85%	95%
Maximize dollar amount of research and development claim	5%	Actual dollar amount of research and development claim ($M)	$ 2.5	$ 3.0
SWAS	10%	Formulated informally, subjectively based on 360 degree feedback	Subjective Score	
Maximize department scorecard score	10%	Actual department scorecard score	---------- N/A ----------	
Maximize organizational scorecard score	10%	Actual organizational scorecard score	---------- N/A ----------	
Total Weight (must = 100%)	**100%**			

mmary

At this point the individual scorecard(s) phase, and thus the initial implementation, is complete. The process is not, however. It is very important at this point to continue to communicate the scorecard through the organization. The scorecard initiative is one that will likely take some time for employees to adjust to; communication will aid greatly in this adjustment. There should also be some mechanism for employees to ask questions and voice concerns, especially those with individual scorecards. Effective change management, discussed later in the book, is crucial to the success of the scorecard initiative. It is strongly recommended that change management techniques be employed wherever applicable. This is so important, it is mentioned at the end of each chapter.

The next step occurs once the fiscal period is complete, and is the entry of actual results into the scorecard to determine whether the objectives set out were achieved. This is the subject of the next chapter.

Chapter 6

Scoring the Balanced Scorecard

Overview

Once the fiscal period is complete and data is available for inputting to the scorecard, scores can be determined for each department scorecard. Scores are a very useful element of the scorecard process — they can provide a wealth of relevant information on how each segment performed compared to initial expectations. It provides excellent insight not only on performance but also on areas for improving the scorecard process, especially in the first couple of years after implementation. This chapter will provide a look at Delphis Mobility's performance by scoring each of the three segments that have had scorecards created thus far: Samantha, the IT Department, and the Delphis Mobility organization.

The Importance of Scoring

The actual construction of a balanced scorecard system can be very useful in gaining understanding regarding how strategy is linked to action. In order to maximize the scorecard's usefulness as a performance measurement system, however, it is imperative that results be gathered and entered into the scorecard in order to gauge how the organization (or department or employee) fared. Without a thorough understanding of actual performance set against initial expectations, it is difficult, if not impossible, to make informed decision-making regarding future action. In addition, the scorecard results can be used as a basis of compensation. This will be demonstrated later in the chapter.

Scoring Frequency

Just like the organization scorecard, the main benefit of the departmental scorecard is to assess how well the department did in achieving the goals set out. First, it needs to be determined how often the scorecard will be scored. Just like the organization scorecard, there are four commonly considered alternatives:

1. Annually,

2. Semi-annually,

3. Quarterly, and

4. Monthly.

An annual scoring process is generally not the most effective, since the greatest benefit of the scorecard is as an indicator of what is going well or not going well. It needs to be assessed at least once during the fiscal year.

Monthly scoring, while ideal from an information standpoint, is simply too time-intensive, given all the effort that goes into the scoring process. Unless an organization is fortunate enough to have the information systems in place to allow for monthly scoring with minimal effort, it is not advised. This is not to say, however, that an "informal" scoring should not take place as a method of understanding performance to date. It is a formal scoring that is not recommended on a monthly basis.

This leaves two alternatives: semi-annually or quarterly. Either of these is acceptable, and it is a judgment call as to which should be used. What will dictate which one is most appropriate will be factors such as:

- The perceived importance of regular scoring;

- The number of staff that need to be involved in the scoring process, and their time availability;

- The ease or lack of ease of the scoring process; and

- Management preference for one or the other.

Another alternative is to try both, one in each of the first two fiscal years of scorecard implementation, then decide which is most appropriate. At some point in the first few years, a firm decision should be made — hopefully the choice will become clear.

Because the scorecard has been set up to facilitate scoring, the actual scoring procedure is composed of three main tasks:

1. Accessing the actual data that will populate the "Actual" column of the scorecard;

2. Entering the data into the scorecard; and

3. Interpreting the score results.

cessing Actual Data

As was mentioned in Chapter 3, development of the scorecard must factor into it the accessibility of actual data. It is pointless creating goals and measures for which no actual useful information exists. In the ideal scenario, the data needed for scorecard scoring will already exist within the information technology currently available at the organization. Simply analyze the data and transfer the results directly into the scorecard. While this may be possible for measures such as total revenue and total profits, the data will have to be manipulated into the scorecard. For example, goals such as increasing new service revenue or maximizing market share may take some more effort, depending on the systems available. By pre-planning the task of data collection during the measure determination stage, the scorecard becomes much easier to score.

tering Actual Data

When measure data becomes available after the fiscal period, the scorecard is ready to have the data entered and to compute scores. It is important at this point to review the measure definitions, so that the actual data entered is aligned with the target and stretch goals entered previously. There are three possible sets of scorecards that will need to have data entered. For each scorecard set, entering actual data for each goal will facilitate calculation of a score for each goal, each perspective, and for the entire scorecard as well. Figure 6-1 provides the financial perspective for the Delphis Mobility organization-level balanced scorecard, with actual results entered. From this, one can establish whether goals were achieved by comparison to the target and stretch goals beside. For example, it is clear that stretch results were achieved for the profit goal, an indication that the fiscal period went very well, at least financially. Figures 6-2, 6-3, and 6-4 provide actual results for the other three perspectives. From these, one can see that there is a wide variance with respect to goal achievement — some are higher than target, some lower. This is to be expected. With this level of analysis, it is difficult, if not impossible, to determine how Delphis Mobility did in an overall sense. With all the puts and takes evident with so many goals, how did the company do on their scorecard overall? This will be addressed in the next section.

Figure 6-1

Delphis Mobility
Financial Perspective
2002

Goals	Weight	Measures	Target	Stretch	Actual
Maximize after-tax profits	25%	Actual after-tax profits ($M)	$ 110.0	$ 130.0	$ 130.0
Maximize ROI	35%	Actual ROI	17%	19%	18%
Minimize cash cycle time	15%	Average number of receivable days	45	40	50
Maximize share price	25%	Actual share price on December 30, 2002	$ 60.00	$ 75.00	$ 60.37
Total Weight (must = 100%)	**100%**				

Figure 6-2

Delphis Mobility
Customer Perspective
2002

Goals	Weight	Measures	Target	Stretch	Actual
Maximize market share	30%	Actual market share %	32.0%	36.0%	33.0%
Maximize customer satisfaction	30%	Customer satisfaction index results	85%	90%	83%
Reduce new phone activation time	20%	Average actual new phone activation time (hours)	13	11	13.5
Minimize 'churn' (lost customer) rate	20%	Actual churn rate	2.0%	1.6%	2.1%
Total Weight (must = 100%)	**100%**				

Figure 6-3

Delphis Mobility
Internal Business Process Perspective
2002

Goals	Weight	Measures	Target	Stretch	Actual
Reduce month end close and reporting cycle time	25%	Actual month end close and reporting time (days)	3.5	3.0	4.0
Increase call range	20%	Actual increase in call range	8%	12%	14%
Minimize number of dropped calls	30%	Actual dropped call percentage	2%	1%	2.2%
Maximize billing accuracy	25%	Actual billing accuracy percentage	99.2%	99.7%	99.5%
Total Weight (must = 100%)	**100%**				

Figure 6-4

Delphis Mobility
Innovation & Learning Perspective
2002

Goals	Weight	Measures	Target	Stretch	Actual
Maximize employee satisfaction ratio	30%	Actual employee satisfaction ratio	84%	90%	86
Maximize retention of best employees	25%	Actual average number of employee years with company	2.5	2.8	2.6
Maximize new billable service revenues	30%	Actual revenues from new billable services ($M)	$ 9.5	$ 11.0	$ 8.8
Increase number of employees certified in project management	15%	Actual percentage of employees certified in project management	20%	25%	16%
Total Weight (must = 100%)	**100%**				

Scoring

While a scan of the balanced scorecard results may offer a hint of how the overall company performance went, one of the best features of a balanced scorecard system is the ability to calculate specific, quantifiable scores for each goal, each perspective, and ultimately the entire balanced scorecard.

There are many ways to calculate scores for a scorecard. Whichever method of scoring is adopted, it should be easy to calculate and understand by those responsible for effecting results. This book uses a scaling factor that calculates scores for goals with a success rate of 60% and 100%. Therefore, a goal with results at the poorest end receives a score of 60% and a perfect score (i.e., stretch) receives a score of 100%. Any results exactly on target receive a score of exactly 80%. Goals that have results somewhere in between receive a prorated score. This scoring system is somewhat arbitrary — a system can use 70% as a target rather than 80%, or a numerical system out of 10 or even 100 for scoring purposes. The important factors that must be inherent in the scoring system are simplicity and understandability. It should also facilitate a simple transition into the compensation scheme, since balanced scorecards are often used for compensation purposes. A demonstration of how the score can be used for compensation will be given later in this chapter.

Note that the scoring method used in this book has a minimum possible of score of 60%, and a maximum score of 100%. A "ceiling" is put on high scores to protect the organization against the possibility of an employee focusing too much effort on a particular goal (normally one with a high weighting) at the possible detriment of other goals. The "floor" value is put on low scores for two reasons. First, so employees can consider the system fair — a ceiling with no floor may be perceived as unfair. Since the ceiling is 20% above target, it seems fair to have a floor exactly 20% below target. Second, a minimum value for goals provides a "safety net" to employees, where an extremely poor performance on one or two goals cannot completely wipe out a decent performance on the rest of their goals. This serves to encourage employees to continue to work toward maximizing their overall scorecard score. It also promotes the fairness of the scorecard to employees, increasing the likelihood of buy-in.

 It is possible to remove the "ceiling" and "floor" discussed above, should the organization wish to avoid these restrictions. The only change that needs to take place is to take off the maximum and minimum score restriction. Encouraging employees to go "beyond stretch" is suitable for many organizations, especially those that find it difficult to set appropriate targets.

eliminary Scoring

Figure 6-5 shows scores for the goals in the financial perspective of the organizational scorecard. Since the actual results for the first goal (profits) is equal to stretch, a score of 100% is awarded. The ROI results were exactly halfway between target and stretch, earning it a score of 90%. The next goal was the cash cycle time goal, where the results were disappointing. A score of 60% was given here since the actual results were below target by exactly the amount of variance between target and stretch (five days). Share price was pretty much right on target, and receives a (rounded) score of 80%. Figures 6-6, 6-7, and 6-8 provide scores for each goal based on the actual results for the other three perspectives.

Figure 6-5

Delphis Mobility
Financial Perspective
2002

Goals	Weight	Measures	Target	Stretch	Actual	Score
Maximize after-tax profits	25%	Actual after-tax profits ($M)	$ 110.0	$ 130.0	$ 130.0	100%
Maximize ROI	35%	Actual ROI	17%	19%	18%	90%
Minimize cash cycle time	15%	Average number of receivable days	45	40	51	60%
Maximize share price	25%	Actual share price on December 30, 2002	$ 60.00	$ 75.00	$ 60.37	80%
Total Weight (must = 100%)	**100%**					

Figure 6-6

Delphis Mobility
Customer Perspective
2002

Goals	Weight	Measures	Target	Stretch	Actual	Score
Maximize market share	30%	Actual market share %	32.0%	36.0%	33.0%	85%
Maximize customer satisfaction	30%	Customer satisfaction index results	85%	90%	83%	72%
Reduce new phone activation time	20%	Average actual new phone activation time (hours)	13	11	13.5	75%
Minimize 'churn' (lost customer) rate	20%	Actual churn rate	2.0%	1.6%	2.1%	75%
Total Weight (must = 100%)	**100%**					

Figure 6-7

Delphis Mobility
Internal Business Process Perspective
2002

Goals	Weight	Measures	Target	Stretch	Actual	Score
Reduce month end close and reporting cycle time	25%	Actual month end close and reporting time (days)	3.5	3.0	4.0	60%
Increase call range	20%	Actual increase in call range	8%	12%	14%	100%
Minimize number of dropped calls	30%	Actual dropped call percentage	2%	1%	2.2%	76%
Maximize billing accuracy	25%	Actual billing accuracy percentage	99.2%	99.7%	99.5%	92%
Total Weight (must = 100%)	**100%**					

Figure 6-8

Delphis Mobility
Innovation & Learning Perspective
2002

Goals	Weight	Measures	Target	Stretch	Actual	Score
Maximize employee satisfaction ratio	30%	Actual employee satisfaction ratio	84%	90%	86%	87%
Maximize retention of best employees	25%	Actual average number of employee years with company	2.5	2.8	2.6	87%
Maximize new billable service revenues	30%	Actual revenues from new billable services ($M)	$ 9.5	$ 11.0	$ 8.8	71%
Increase number of employees certified in project	15%	Actual percentage of employees certified in project	20%	25%	16%	64%
Total Weight (must = 100%)	**100%**					

ighted Scoring

At this point each goal has its own score. In order to calculate a score for each entire perspective, it is necessary to factor in the weights that have been assigned to each goal. The next step then is to calculate weighted scores, based on the weights applied during the scorecard creation process. This is accomplished simply by multi-plying the assigned weight with the related goal score. Figure 6-9 provides a financial perspective scoring detail complete with weighted scores for each goal. The perspective score is computed by adding up all the weighted scores. The scoring system for the perspective is the same as that for goals (80% equates to target, etc.). One can see that Delphis Mobility has done quite well in the financial perspective. Figures 6-10, 6-11, and 6-12 provide weighted scores for each goal plus a perspective score for the other three perspectives. One can see that the results for the other three perspectives are mixed and less stellar than the financial perspective.

Figure 6-9

Delphis Mobility
Financial Perspective
2002

Goals	Weight	Measures	Target	Stretch	Actual	Score	Weighted Score
Maximize after-tax profits	25%	Actual after-tax profits ($M)	$ 110.0	$ 130.0	$ 130.0	100%	25%
Maximize ROI	35%	Actual ROI	17%	19%	18%	90%	32%
Minimize cash cycle time	15%	Average number of receivable days	45	40	51	60%	9%
Maximize share price	25%	Actual share price on December 30, 2002	$ 60.00	$ 75.00	$ 60.37	80%	20%

Total Weight (must = 100%)	100%				Financial Perspective Score:	86%

Figure 6-10

Delphis Mobility
Customer Perspective
2002

Goals	Weight	Measures	Target	Stretch	Actual	Score	Weighted Score
Maximize market share	30%	Actual market share %	32.0%	36.0%	33.0%	85%	26%
Maximize customer satisfaction	30%	Customer satisfaction index results	85%	90%	83%	72%	22%
Reduce new phone activation time	20%	Average actual new phone activation time (hours)	13	11	13.5	75%	15%
Minimize 'churn' (lost customer) rate	20%	Actual churn rate	2.0%	1.6%	2.1%	75%	15%
Total Weight (must = 100%)	**100%**			**Customer Perspective Score:**			**77%**

Figure 6-11

Delphis Mobility
Internal Business Process Perspective
2002

Goals	Weight	Measures	Target	Stretch	Actual	Score	Weighted Score
Reduce month end close and reporting cycle time	25%	Actual month end close and reporting time (days)	3.5	3.0	4.0	60%	15%
Increase call range	20%	Actual increase in call range	8%	12%	14%	100%	20%
Minimize number of dropped calls	30%	Actual dropped call percentage	2%	1%	2.2%	76%	23%
Maximize billing accuracy	25%	Actual billing accuracy percentage	99.2%	99.7%	99.5%	92%	23%
Total Weight (must = 100%)	**100%**		**Internal Business Process Perspective Score:**				**81%**

Figure 6-12

Delphis Mobility
Innovation & Learning Perspective
2002

Goals	Weight	Measures	Target	Stretch	Actual	Score	Weighted Score
Maximize employee satisfaction ratio	30%	Actual employee satisfaction ratio	84%	90%	86	87%	26%
Maximize retention of best employees	25%	Actual average number of employee years with company	2.5	2.8	2.6	87%	22%
Maximize new billable service revenues	30%	Actual revenues from new billable services ($M)	$ 9.5	$ 11.0	$ 8.8	71%	21%
Increase number of employees certified in project management	15%	Actual percentage of employees certified in project management	20%	25%	16%	64%	10%
Total Weight (must = 100%)	**100%**	Innovation & Learning Perspective Score:					**79%**

The final score that must be calculated for the organization-level balanced score-card is an overall score. This can be calculated by multiplying the perspective score by the perspective weights that were assigned during the scorecard construction process. Figure 6-13 shows that Delphis Mobility received an overall score of exactly 80%. This can be considered a good score, since 80% represents target.

Figure 6-13

Delphis Mobility
Overall Balanced Scorecard Summary
2002

	Weighting	Perspective Score	Weighted Score
Financial	20%	86%	17%
Customer	30%	77%	23%
Internal Business Process	30%	81%	24%
Innovation & Learning	20%	79%	16%
Total	100%		80.0%

oring and the Department Scorecard

At this point actual results data has been entered into the organization-level scorecard, facilitating scoring at all levels of the scorecard. The same process should be repeated for the department-level scorecard. Like the organization scorecard, the score range in the departmental scorecard is anywhere from 60% to 100%, with 80% being the "on-target" indicator score. Figures 6-14 to 6-17 provide the score results for each of the IT Department's four perspectives: financial (Figure 6-14); customer (Figure 6-15); internal business (Figure 6-16); and innovation and learning (Figure 6-17). Figure 6-18 demonstrates an overall score for the IT Department. One can see that because of the poor showing for IT in the customer perspective, the overall department score is below 80% — this in spite of the fact that three of four perspectives had a positive score. This is a strong indication of how important the weighting process is — because the customer perspective was weighted quite high, it pulled the overall score down below 80%.

Figure 6-14

Delphis Mobility
IT Department
Financial Perspective
2002

Goals	Weight	Measures	Target	Stretch	Actual	Score	Weighted Score
Minimize spending on technology, while maintaining system integrity	35%	Actual dollar spend (vs. benchmark, in $M)	$ 40	$ 38	$ 39	90%	32%
Minimize number of new hires, while maintaining system integrity	30%	Actual number of hires (vs. benchmark)	20	15	22	72%	22%
Minimize discretionary IT expenditures	20%	Actual dollar spend (vs. benchmark, in $M)	$ 5	$ 4	$ 5.5	70%	14%
Maximize savings through activity analysis and waste reduction	15%	Total demonstrated savings (in $M)	$ 3	$ 4	$ 4	100%	15%

| Total Weight (must = 100%) | 100% | | | Financial Perspective Score: | | | 82% |

Figure 6-15

Delphis Mobility
IT Department
Customer Perspective
2002

Goals	Weight	Measures	Target	Stretch	Actual	Score	Weighted Score
Provide accurate, timely market data	20%	Actual accuracy, timeliness of market data	97%	99%	98%	90%	18%
Provide accurate, timely customer data	20%	Actual accuracy, timeliness of customer data	98%	99%	97%	60%	12%
Optimize business management affiliations	20%	Actual internal customer survey results	80%	90%	83%	86%	17%
Optimize Customer Service affiliation	15%	Actual internal customer survey results	85%	90%	82%	68%	10%
Maximize satisfaction level of internal customer departments	25%	Actual internal customer survey results	85%	88%	84%	73%	18%

Total Weight (must = 100%)	100%		Customer Perspective Score:	76%

Figure 6-16

Delphis Mobility
IT Department
Internal Business Perspective
2002

Goals	Weight	Measures	Target	Stretch	Actual	Score	Weighted Score
Maximize system usefulness for reporting purposes	20%	Actual satisfaction survey results	85%	95%	87%	84%	17%
Minimize billing system downtime	15%	Actual total hours of downtime	100	80	110	70%	11%
Optimize billing engine inspection frequency	10%	Total number of inspections	24	26	23	70%	7%
Minimize activation gateway downtime	20%	Actual total hours of downtime	75	60	70	87%	17%
Minimize activation process cycle time	20%	Average actual cycle time on November 30, 2002	13	11	14	70%	14%
Reduce cycle time of departmental project approval process	15%	Actual average cycle time (days)	1.5	1.0	1.0	100%	15%

Total Weight (must = 100%)	100%	Internal Business Perspective Score:	81%

Figure 6-17

Delphis Mobility
IT Department
Innovation & Learning Perspective
2002

Goals	Weight	Measures	Target	Stretch	Actual	Score	Weighted Score
Maximize number of marketable services developed	30%	Actual number of marketable services developed	2	4	3	90%	27%
Maximize employee satisfaction ratio	35%	Actual employee satisfaction ratio	80%	90%	85%	90%	32%
Further enhance/develop IT-related skills as necessary	20%	Total average number of approved training days per employee	4	5	3	60%	12%
Assist HR with meeting certified project manager targets	15%	Number of certified project managers in IT	30	35	27	68%	10%
Total Weight (must = 100%)	**100%**	Innovation & Learning Perspective Score:					**81%**

Figure 6-18

Delphis Mobility
IT Department
Overall Balanced Scorecard Summary
2002

	Weighting	Perspective Score	Weighted Score
Financial Perspective	20%	82%	16%
Customer Perspective	35%	76%	26%
Internal Business Perspective	25%	81%	20%
Innovation & Learning Perspective	20%	81%	16%
Total	**100%**		**79.2%**

oring and the Individual Scorecard

The final set of scorecards to complete are the individual scorecards. The process is quite similar to the organization-level and department-level scorecards, actually a bit easier since there are no perspectives to score. Figure 6-19 provides a scored scorecard for Samantha, who received an overall score of 82%.

Figure 6-19

Individual Balanced Scorecard
Delphis Mobility
IT Department
2002

Employee Name: Samantha

Goals	Weight	Measures	Target	Stretch	Actual	Score	Weighted Score
Minimize number of new hires, while maintaining system integrity	10%	Actual number of new hires	10	8	7	100%	10%
Maximize accuracy and timeliness of project proposal documentation	10%	Percentage of project proposals submitted accurately and on time	90%	95%	87%	68%	7%
Maximize internal customer satisfaction index	20%	Actual internal customer satisfaction index score	90%	95%	90%	80%	16%
Increase/develop employee skills	5%	Percentage of employees that obtain project management or other approved certification	95%	98%	87%	60%	3%
Increase/develop employee skills	5%	Percentage of employees that attend company's 'internal customer service' course	95%	100%	98%	92%	5%
Increase employee satisfaction index	15%	Actual employee satisfaction index score	85%	95%	88%	86%	13%
Maximize dollar amount of research and development claim	5%	Actual dollar amount of research and development claim ($M)	$ 2.5	$ 3.0	$ 2.8	92%	5%
SWAS	10%	Formulated informally, subjectively based on 360 degree feedback	---------- N/A ----------			83%	8%
Maximize department scorecard score	10%	Actual department scorecard score	---------- N/A ----------			79.2%	8%
Maximize organizational scorecard score	10%	Actual organizational scorecard score	---------- N/A ----------			80.0%	8%
Total Weight (must = 100%)	**100%**				Samantha Score:		**82%**

> ☞ **Do not be afraid to adjust targets, or stretch goals or weights to create a revised score that intuitively is more reflective of an employee's, department's, or organization's performance. For example, if an employee makes a strong effort but, due to circumstances outside his/her control, the scorecard score indicates performance was below expectation, some adjustments should be made to reflect the individual's efforts. While, ideally, the need to make such adjustments should be minimized, it is paramount that employees perceive the scorecard system as a fair way of assessing overall performance. This factor should take priority over the need for "accurate" scoring. If the scorecard system is perceived as unjust by employees, it will have a very limited life.**

Linking the Scorecard to Compensation

One of the most useful features of the balanced scorecard is the fact that it can be used to calculate an employee's bonus in a more objective fashion than most other reward systems. If the initiative has been executed properly, the score on an employee's scorecard should be a reflection of how well they have helped (or hindered) the organization toward achieving its objectives. That said, it makes sense to link the score on the scorecard to an employee's performance bonus. The fact that the score is numerical makes this even simpler.

Figure 6-20
Individual Scorecard Compensation
Delphis Mobility
IT Department
2002

Employee Name: Samantha

Compensation Scheme:

Stretch Bonus Compensation:	$5,000
Score:	82%
Total Bonus Compensation:	**$4,106**

There are several ways of linking the scorecard to compensation. One possibility is to take the score on the employee's scorecard and use it as a bonus multiplier. The first task that must be performed using this method is the determination of what a target bonus should be. In other words, if an employee were to achieve a score exactly equal to target (i.e., 80%), what should their bonus be? Human Resources should be involved in making this determination where applicable. Or perhaps a target bonus has already been established. It could be a percentage of salary or some other method used to arrive at the amount. It is necessary to complete this step before moving forward.

Figure 6-20 provides a possible bonus calculation for Samantha. With a stretch bonus of $5,000 established, the actual payout is just this amount multiplied by the actual score. This is just one of many possible ways to compute a bonus. There is no one best method of linking the scorecard to compensation — the items to keep in mind when making this decision are:

- Simplicity (it must be understandable to employees);

- The rough dollar amounts the organization wants to award for certain scorecard scores; and

- The most appropriate amount for a target bonus.

The compensation portion of the scorecard will likely require refinement over time. This fact should be communicated to employees. Also, the importance of Human Resources in this particular segment of the scorecard system cannot be overstated.

Another topic worthy of discussion is whether compensation needs to be linked to the scorecard at all. The simple answer is: no. The balanced scorecard can be a very useful tool in raising employee morale, simply because many employees will feel (possibly for the first time) that their job is directly related to and linked with the organization's strategy. They may feel that the intrinsic reward of knowing they have made a difference is enough to merit their complete buy-in to the balanced scorecard system.

Many, however, may not feel quite the same motivation. They may decide that, if they are performing at or above expectations based on their scorecard results, they should be compensated accordingly. So while the short answer to whether compensation must be linked to the scorecard is no, the fact is, establishing the linkage is much more likely to gain across-the-board buy-in. Whether people are intrinsically motivated by the scorecard, extrinsically motivated, or perhaps both, linking the scorecard to compensation will result in a scorecard that caters to them in some way.

☞ **Evidence suggests that when any new system is tied into employee compensation, it tends to gain much more attention by employees. The balanced scorecard is a tool that requires a vast amount of attention paid to it, which suggests that tying compensation to the scorecard makes sense. Most balanced scorecard organizations have linked compensation to the scorecard.**

☞ **Compensation can be tied into scorecard results achieved in other related scorecards. For example, an element of the employee's scorecard might be the results of the department or team scorecard to which that employee belongs. This is a way of tying individual compensation to team or group performance, thus encouraging teamwork and cross-functional cooperation.**

Summary

With the scoring process complete after the end of the fiscal period, it is time to reflect on the entire implementation process and make any modifications or enhancements necessary to make the scorecard system the best possible. The entire scorecard process can really be considered a work in progress for at least the first couple of years after implementation. It is imperative to solicit feedback and suggestions for improvement, deal with employee concerns, and make changes as necessary. The balanced scorecard is an excellent system of performance management, as long as continuous improvement is factored in.

Chapter 7

Other Scorecard Considerations

Overview

To this point in the book, a fairly generic approach has been taken with regard to scorecard implementation. Of course the fact is, all organizations are different and as a result, implementation of a balanced scorecard initiative will raise different issues in different organizations and some important considerations merit discussion. The topics that will be given consideration in this chapter are:

- Use of a surrogate scorecard;
- The administration/relation tradeoff;
- The lag phenomenon;
- Employee resistance;
- Goal setting and benchmarking;
- Defining measures;
- Measure data availability;
- Software; and
- Common pitfalls.

Each item mentioned above will be discussed in detail. No specific prescribed course of action will be given since each organizational circumstance is different and judgment calls must be made based on the circumstances. Rather, the discussion will focus on the most important elements of each topic, which should be helpful in making the appropriate judgment call. Where appropriate, suggested courses of action will be made.

Use of a Surrogate Scorecard

Frequently, a department head will want to implement a balanced scorecard, but is in the unfortunate position of not having an organizational level scorecard from which to cascade. The creation of a departmental scorecard is still possible however, through the use of a surrogate scorecard. A surrogate scorecard is a fictitious organizational level scorecard created for the sole purpose of cascading. By brainstorming a list of organizational goals and following Steps 1 and 2 from Chapter 3, a decent surrogate scorecard can be created.

When creating the surrogate scorecard, it is likely that managers at the department-level will be the main contributors — top management will likely have little or no input. It is important then for department level managers to create the surrogate scorecard from an organizational perspective. If too much departmental bias creeps into surrogate scorecard, it will not be as effective. So it is important to take the "department hat" off, and put the "CEO hat" on; the goals need to be at the organizational level. The tools to create these goals are the same as in Chapter 2.

Since the surrogate scorecard will not actually be scored at any time, it is not necessary to create measures and weights for it. It is also not imperative to strive for the same level of perfection that would be sought in a true organizational scorecard scenario. Once the goals for each perspective have been established and the scorecard is reasonably balanced, it is ready to be cascaded on.

While the ideal scenario would consist of an actual organizational scorecard, the surrogate scorecard is a useful tool to allow departments to implement a scorecard, rather than using no scorecard at all. Perhaps success at the departmental level can act as a springboard to organization-wise scorecard implementation.

 While the balanced scorecard does not lend itself well to piloting, a surrogate scorecard may be an ideal way to pilot the scorecard.

Administration/Relation Tradeoff

Thus far in the book, a framework for cascading the scorecard down to the lower levels of the organization has been described. However, very few organizations will want to cascade down to the level where all employees have their own personal scorecard. Indeed, few will even benefit from this. Ideally each employee could have their own scorecard to maximize the likelihood that they can relate to the scorecard (i.e., their relation to the scorecard). Speaking practically however, the cost in administration of supplying each and every employee a scorecard would not be worth it in most cases (small organizations are often an exception). That said, the issue then becomes, to what level should the scorecard be cascaded (i.e., where is the administration — relation tradeoff point)? This question must be answered — there is no way around it.

Figure 7-1

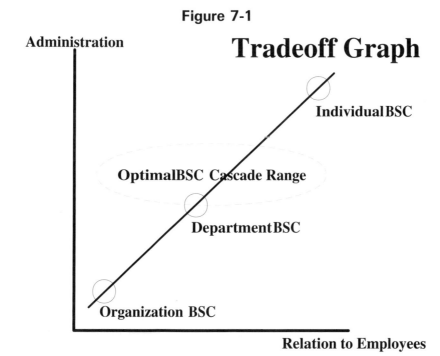

While there is no simple answer to this question, there are a couple of alternatives to consider that may assist with the judgment call that will ensue. At minimum they provide an excellent starting point for making the tradeoff decision.

Most organizations can be divided a couple of different ways — these may provide the starting point for making the administration/relation tradeoff decision. The first way many organizations are divided is between management and non-management. There is often some threshold or grade where a certain level is considered management; the level immediately below is considered non-management. This may provide the ideal tradeoff point, or at least a starting point. Usually the expectation is that employees in a management role are decision-makers, compensated to execute strategy, and thus merit having their own scorecard. In an age of empowerment, it may also be that certain employees in a technically non-management role are also decision-makers and thus merit their own scorecards; Thus, the management/non-management division can provide an excellent starting point.

Another common division in organizations is a split between those who receive additional compensation based on performance and those who do not (this may or may not be the same split as the management/non-management split discussed above). As stated, linking the individual scorecard to compensation is important so cascading the scorecard to those who receive performance-based compensation may provide the tradeoff point. Or like the split discussed earlier, it may provide a starting point in making the tradeoff decision. It could be that employees not previously compensated based on performance will now be as part of the balanced scorecard initiative. In this case, the split may provide the starting point in determining which employees to add to the performance-based compensation plan.

As indicated earlier, the point where the benefit of an employee having a scorecard is deemed not to be worth the additional scorecard administration is a judgment call. A couple of alternatives have been provided which will affords the decision-maker a starting point in making this tradeoff. Two more points are worthy of note here. First, in making this decision, it is much wiser to err on the side of too few employees cascaded than too many. If it turns out that too few were chosen, there is always the ability to add more employees later. This approach minimizes the complexity in the initial stages and allows subsequent cascade efforts to run smoother, based on the lessons learned in the initial rollout. Second, if too many employees are chosen for cascading it could produce undesired results and threaten the success of the initiative. Figure 7.1 provides an graphical view of the administration/relation tradeoff. From this figure one can see that, while pinpointing the exact level of cascade may difficult, it generally will be at some point just below the departmental level. In other words, each department should have their own scorecard. The appropriateness of individuals within the department having their own scorecard is the real decision area.

The Lag Phenomenon

Any initiative will have an initial period of investment, followed by planned benefits of some kind. At some point a payback period is expected to be realized, where the benefits of the project meet and then surpass the initial investment. The balanced scorecard is no different. What tends to separate a balanced scorecard initiative from most other types of initiatives is the fact that the payback period can be much longer. The "lag phenomenon" is a term to describe the long time period between implementing a balanced scorecard initiative and realizing the payback period. It is referred to as a phenomenon since usually this period is much longer than an organization expects, and has been responsible for the abandonment of many scorecard initiatives. It is therefore an extremely important topic of discussion, so that potential scorecard adopters can understand and plan for this lag period. The fact still remains that, despite the longer payback period, a well implemented scorecard can reap benefits well into the future.

The lag phenomenon happens for three main reasons:

1. The high initial cost of implementation;

2. The decrease in employee productivity as they adjust to their new roles and expectations; and

3. The fact that often employees earn scorecard bonuses well before the organization has yielded the desired financial results.

Each reason will be discussed below.

High Implementation Cost

Like most initiatives, there are both internal and external costs to implementation. The bulk of the external costs fall mainly to consulting and software, should a software solution be used. Like any other strategic implementation, the degree to which consultants and software are used will be determined within the organization, based on factors such as budget, access to consultants, etc.

Costs likely to run higher than would be expected would fall within the realm of internal costs. The fact is, in its initial stages a balanced scorecard initiative requires a massive amount of brainstorming that must be performed by internal employees who know the company (i.e., a consultant can facilitate a brainstorming session, nothing more). The amount of effort required by internal resources can run high, and will account for a high internal cost that must be planned for. These high costs of implementation contribute to the lag phenomenon.

Employee Productivity Decrease

Many employees will be faced with their regular tasks changing as a result of a balanced scorecard implementation. For these employees, there will be a period of decreased productivity as they adjust to their new roles and learn new activities (often referred to as the learning curve). This productivity decrease is generally unavoidable, but can be minimized through proper communication and training. Unfortunately, it will result in some level of lost productivity toward the beginning of the balanced scorecard initiative, and therefore contributes to the lag phenomenon.

Bonuses

It was explained in Chapter 1 how success in each of the customer, internal business, and innovation and learning perspectives will ultimately lead to desired results in the financial perspective. The additional returns in the financial perspective will almost always be at some point after success in the other three perspectives. In other words, an organization needs to do well in the non-financial perspectives for financial success to be realized from the scorecard initiative. That said, consider that most of an employee's scorecard-related bonus is likely to be for non-financial-related goals. In other words, an employee can "cash in" by scoring high on their scorecard (thus meriting a bonus) long before the organization has realized any financial success from the scorecard initiative. This can create the undesirable situation where an organization has a large pool of bonuses owing but no cash to support it.

Fortunately, there are strategies to deal with the lag phenomenon. Keep in mind also that this situation is temporary — if the balanced scorecard initiative has been implemented properly, the fact that employees are earning bonuses means that they are taking the appropriate action, and financial results will follow. There are three strategies that can assist in dealing with this temporary circumstance:

1. Adopting a deferred bonus plan;

2. Using shares instead of cash; and

3. Heavy weighting toward the organizational financial perspective initially.

Deferred Bonus Plan

When an employee earns a bonus and when they are paid are usually two different time periods. In the early era of a balanced scorecard implementation, it may be useful to negotiate with employees some form of deferred bonus plan, where they will be paid the bonus they have earned at some later date. Or alternatively, they could be paid a fraction up front with the balance being paid at some later date. This will often be acceptable to employees if the rationale behind this scheme is communicated well. In addition, attaching interest to unpaid bonus balances will be much more palatable to employees. This can help in dealing with the bonus timing issue.

Issuing Shares

For companies that have the option of issuing shares, an alternative that may be available is to award employees company shares in lieu of cash. This of course would avoid the need to come up with the cash that would be necessary otherwise. Some might be reluctant to consider this option since any shares issued will dilute both the ownership of each share as well as the earnings per share. While this is true, if employees are earning scorecard bonuses it means that they are actually doing those things that should ultimately make both the overall profitability and value of the company rise. So it seems quite feasible that any increase in shares may be more than offset by additional profits and company value. In addition, the cash that is freed up by issuing shares can be put to use generating further cash-flow. So the issuance of shares is something that might be considered to aid in dealing with the bonus timing issue.

avy Weighting Toward the Organizational Scorecard

It was recommended in Chapter 5 that an element of both departmental and organizational scorecard scores be included on each and every individual scorecard as a mechanism of promoting teamwork and unity. It can also assist in dealing with the lag phenomenon. If necessary, an organization can do two things to align the employee's bonus with organizational results:

1. On the employee's scorecard, apply additional weighting to the organizational scorecard score (e.g., if the long-term plan for the employee scorecard is a weight of 10% for organizational scores, make it 20%).

2. On the organizational scorecard, make the weight of the financial perspective higher (e.g., if the long-term plan for the financial perspective is a weight of 20%, make it 40%).

One must be very cautious in using this approach — if an employee feels that their scorecard score is largely determined by activities out of their control, it may result in a lack of motivation. If this approach is used, it should be communicated that these particular weightings are short term and that in the future the employee will be more of a determinant in the individual scorecard results.

e Lag Phenomenon: Summary

The lag phenomenon must be expected to a certain degree — failure to recognize this at the outset can be perilous in that it will create unexpected and disappointing scorecard results. Recognizing it and using one or more of the above strategies to deal with it will maximize the likelihood of a successful scorecard implementation.

ployee Resistance

A balanced scorecard, like any other initiative, is at some point destined to meet with employees who will not be fully supportive of the implementation. It is an unfortunate but very real fact that, generally speaking, people do not embrace change very well. Change tends to bring people out of their comfort zones, especially when they do not know or understand the changes that will be brought about. Often the reason is a very rational fear of what the new initiative will bring to the individual. Examples of fears are job loss (theirs or others), demotion (real or virtual) or a reduced bonus. Employees may agree with the initiative in principle and want to fully participate. The threat of change however (real or imagined), can lead some to resist and even sabotage a new initiative. Fear of change and employee resistance must be considered and planned for at the beginning of a balanced scorecard implementation. Change management principles must be employed during a balanced scorecard initiative.

A full and complete discussion on change management principles is beyond the scope of this book. It is recommended that other sources on change management be sought and employed during the balanced scorecard initiative. The remainder of the discussion here regarding overcoming employee resistance will be those few crucial elements of change management that must be employed in order to maximize the likelihood of a successful implementation. Failure to recognize the importance of these items could prove disastrous to the initiative. The elements that will be discussed are:

1. Communicating the balanced scorecard initiative;

2. Seeking employee input; and

3. Addressing employee questions and concerns.

Communicating the Balanced Scorecard Initiative

Once the decision has been made to go forward with a scorecard initiative, it is important to immediately begin devising a communication plan for employees. The actual communication need not start immediately but should commence sometime shortly after initiating the project. There are several vehicles of communication that can be employed; whichever mode is chosen should provide information to all employees affected by the initiative.

It is also important to continue with the communication, particularly as the date of the first rollout approaches. Employees deserve to know about the scorecard, its benefits, and how it will affect their roles with the organization.

 Many organizations regularly post scorecard results throughout the organization. The positive effects of this on communication are two-fold: first, it communicates the fact that management is serious enough about the scorecard to dedicate resources to having results posted; and second, it allows all employees to regularly see and understand how the organization is performing against targets.

Seeking Employee Input

Employee input is a vital ingredient to the scorecard initiative. Failure to recognize this can lead to both a lower quality scorecard and an increase in employee resistance. Employees should feel that they are part of the process, which will increase the likelihood of their buy-in. In addition, the input they provide is most likely to enhance the scorecard. So it is very logical then that employee input should be solicited.

Addressing Employee Questions and Concerns

An ideal scorecard implementation will provide some sort of forum for employees to speak on any issue they might have regarding the scorecard implementation. The comments provided could be positive (e.g., a suggestion) or negative (e.g., a complaint regarding compensation), or somewhat neutral. In any case, the comments should be considered important and somehow incorporated into the final scorecard product. For any employee insights not followed up on, an explanation should be provided to the employee who raised the issue.

Employee Resistance: Summary

Employee resistance needs to be anticipated and proactively dealt with. The strategies discussed above will likely go a long way in assisting with minimizing the impacts of resistance. Other change management techniques should also be employed as necessary to maximize the likelihood of scorecard success.

al Setting and Benchmarking

As discussed early in the book, a strong set of goals is an essential ingredient to a successful balanced scorecard initiative. In fact, the success of the entire initiative can often be determined by the quality of the goals used. The term quality here has many elements: realism, comprehensiveness, measurability and specificity are among the most vital characteristics of quality for balanced scorecard purposes. It is recommended that when the organization is in doubt regarding the realism of a certain goal, they consider benchmarking to assist them. Benchmarking for the purposes of the balanced scorecard can be considered to mean a check for realism through comparison to another entity. For example, an organization may want to provide the Accounts Receivable Department specific target and stretch goals for the average number of days of receivables outstanding, but not know what a good average really is. It can then look to other organizations (and/or divisions within the organization) to see what theirs is. This can help in two key ways:

1. It provides a background or standard for establishing targets, based on what others have actually achieved; and

2. It can assist in taking some of the unnecessary negotiating and emotion out of target-setting — since targets have been set based on real-life examples, it becomes more difficult for employees to consider them unfair.

Benchmarking can be a strategic initiative unto itself, but it does not need to be. The organization can collect information from other organizations just for certain goals if they want to minimize the amount of effort that is put into this segment of the scorecard initiative. The research does not need to be time-consuming or expensive. Benchmarking websites exist that provide specific and relevant information for a fee. Reams of information are also available at no charge via annual reports or Internet web pages. Alternatively, the organization can involve itself in a more formal benchmarking initiative by partnering with other organizations. Benchmarking can be a very beneficial "extra ingredient" in the scorecarding process — it is recommended that it be considered.

> ☞ **The Internet is an excellent resource for benchmarking. Many organizations post their financial results there, and often give strong indications of what their non-financial objectives are. In addition, many balanced scorecard organizations (usually non-profit) proudly post their balanced scorecards on the Internet.**

ining Measures

The discussion of measures thus far has assumed that there is one specific definition for each measure chosen. This is in fact far from the truth. A measure can have many definitions, and it is very important to define each measure so that there are no misunderstandings when the time comes to score each scorecard. A good example of a measure that could have many definitions is on-time delivery. Exactly when should a delivery be considered on time? A three-day delivery may achieve the organization's on-time delivery goals, but if the customer wants it in two days it is not on time by their standards. So it is very important to establish exactly how each measure will be defined for the balanced scorecard.

As a general rule, whenever possible measures should be outcome-based (i.e., based on actual results) rather than input-based. An excellent example of this is with skills development. Often the measure for skills development will be related to the training employees have received (e.g., the number of training days). There is nothing at all wrong with this. Whenever applicable though, a superior measure is some link to the use of the new skill. For example, if a measure can be established that captures how an employee uses the new skills they have learned, this would be superior to a measure that captures only the fact that they have been sent for the training. Unfortunately, this is not always possible.

The importance of strong, well-defined measures is crucial to the ultimate success of the balanced scorecard initiative. The organization needs to recognize this and spend the time and effort to establish a strong set of measures.

Measure Data Availability

To this point in the book, the discussion of measures has generally been done without reference to the fact that data may not be available to objectively determine whether a goal has been achieved. Indeed, it would ideal if a computer program could generate all the measure data necessary with a few commands. Realistically however, not all measures will have data that would be this easy to generate. Often measure data is very difficult to pull together, or is not available at all. For example, quality is frequently used as a scorecard measure. Some quality information may be available. Due to its subjective nature however, often quality will be a judgment call by management and therefore cannot be obtained through objective means. Fortunately, lack of measure data does not preclude a measure from inclusion on the balanced scorecard.

When measure data does not exist, it is appropriate to use a subjective scoring approach in order to come up with a score for that particular goal. Lack of measure data should not be the sole determinant in choosing the appropriate measures for the scorecard — data availability is just one criterion of what constitutes the best measure for any given goal. It is often better to choose a relevant measure that must be scored subjectively than to choose an inappropriate measure simply because the data currently exists for it. A good example of this is a goal oriented toward cycle-time reduction. An obvious measure for this goal is actual cycle time; however, few systems provide this for all processes. This does not mean the measure should be abandoned. Instead, an alternative should be considered for collection of actual cycle-time data (perhaps following a material or invoice through the process) with a subjective or manual score being imposed based on the results.

Figure 7-2 provides an example of a subjective scoring sheet that can be used in the absence of measure data. This sheet or something similar can be used for many goals where measure data does not exist. Again, it is better to choose the best measure available and score it subjectively than it is to use a poor measure simply because data is available for it.

Figure 7-2

Individual Balanced Scorecard —
Subjective Score Worksheet

Employee:
Goal:

This sheet may prove useful in situations where no hard data can be obtained for measurement purposes. In these cases, the scoring must be determined by a more subjective nature, determining by opinion if the employee did or did not do those tasks and key performance indicators that were necessary to achieve the goal in question.

One of these sheets should be used for each instance of a goal score being determined subjectively, and MUST contain employee input.

The scale to be used for these circumstances is as follows:

-2 - Extremely poor effort, results
-1 - Poor effort, results
0 - Effort, results on target
1 - Strong effort, results
2 - Extremely strong effort, results

Scores should be to one decimal (i.e. 1.5 is an acceptable score)

Positive actions the employee took toward achieving this goal:
1)
2)
3)
4)

Negative actions the employee took against achieving this goal:
1)
2)
3)
4)

Any other commentary useful in determining what an appropriate score should be:
1)
2)
3)
4)

Overall, on a scale from -2 to +2, for this goal the employee deserves a score of:

tware

Like many initiatives, several software packages exist that can assist greatly with the balanced scorecard implementation. Indeed, a simple Internet search just completed using the search terms "balanced scorecard software" yielded over 23,000 sites!

By adding the term "English", that list was reduced to about 2,500 — still equating to an incredible number of options for the consumer. The point is, there is no shortage of software packages or vendors that will say that their software is "the" solution. Given the improving quality and decreasing prices of balanced scorecard software, a software solution is highly recommended for most organizations. There are several considerations that should be factored into a final software decision. These considerations are:

1. Implementation budget,

2. Timing of software purchase, and

3. Software fit with specific needs.

Implementation Budget

Like any project, the balanced scorecard implementation must be managed under the constraint of limited resources, namely funding and human resources. This becomes a very important factor in choosing a software solution. Like most software solutions, balanced scorecard software can provide a range of options to suit every budget. There are several cheaper solutions with limited functionality. There are also many expensive versions that have exceptional functionality (often more functionality than will ever be used). It is recommended that as part of the initial planning, an organization decide approximately how much it would be willing to spend on software. This will assist in narrowing the option of solutions. Another consideration that should be kept in mind is the project budget for ongoing maintenance after implementation. Any balanced scorecard implementation will require some staff to maintain and track the scorecard system. Some software packages are better than others at reducing the need for human resources for maintenance and tracking. This should be factored in to the final software decision.

Software Purchase Timing

It is quite common to decide on a software solution before an implementation "goes live". Indeed, it is often necessary to have the software purchased and fully functional as part of a project implementation. It is possible in certain situations to actually allow a project to go live without purchased software. In other words, it may be possible to start an implementation without proprietary software by using common PC tools such as spreadsheet and word processing packages. This could prove advantageous to many organizations that for various reasons may not want to, or be able to, purchase software in the early stages of a balanced scorecard implementation. For example, an organization may just not have the funds to purchase software, but wants to implement a balanced scorecard anyway. This may be an appropriate alternative. Another example is an organization that plans on purchasing software at some point but is not prepared to commit to any one solution. An internal spreadsheet and/or word processing package may be an appropriate short-term solution.

If this internal solution alternative is utilized, the balanced scorecard team should be charged with the responsibility of providing the spreadsheet and/or word processing package solution (of course, they may require assistance from non-team members). Some consultants will provide this type of solution as part of their implementation services. This type of solution can be very effective in ensuring that all team members understand the balanced scorecard process, since a great deal of thought must go into the creation of the short-term solution. A software purchase solution can then by revisited at some future point in time.

While it is recommended that a software solution be considered up front, those organizations that have decided against purchasing software are still encouraged to adopt a scorecard system with an alternative approach, and then consider software at a later point in time.

tware Fit

It is often the case that a software solution seems to cover most of the organization's requirements, and the organization will mold its initiative to fit the rest of the software solution. While this may be fine for some types of software, organizations should be extremely careful not to purchase a balanced scorecard software solution that is a poor fit with the organization. The balanced scorecard is a tool that impacts many people throughout the organization (i.e., it is not a "behind-the-scenes" initiative). It is therefore recommended that software be screened carefully to ensure a fit exists with the entire organization. The organization should first determine its own specific needs, then seek software that will cater to these needs. The better the fit with the organization's specific needs, the higher the likelihood of employee buy-in and ultimate success. The alternative of deferring a software purchase through an internal solution was discussed above — this principle ties in nicely with the principle of fit. Using an internal solution can afford the organization the time needed to nail down specific requirements, then seek a software package that caters to these. A quality internal solution can work indefinitely until the organization finds that required software fit.

In conclusion, a software package is definitely recommended as a tool that will assist greatly in the balanced scorecard implementation. When the software should be purchased is a major issue. Which specific package to purchase also merits much consideration. A fair amount of time in the planning process should be committed to these decisions, so that the software solution ultimately chosen becomes an enabler, not a detriment, to the scorecard initiative.

mmon Pitfalls

Like any initiative, a balanced scorecard can face an early demise if certain hazards are not respected and given proper attention. Some of the ones to look out for and avoid are:

1. A scorecard that applies to senior management only;

2. A set of KPFs that are not linked to strategy;

3. Too many measures;

4. The scorecard becoming "just another report"; and

5. A scorecard that has not incorporated employee participation.

A Scorecard that Applies to Senior Management Only

All too often the scorecard is constructed at the executive level with the assistance of consultants. To make matters worse, communication regarding the scorecard is minimal or even non-existent. In other words, about two or three percent of the organization's employees were involved in the process, which is very close to zero percent of those charged with strategy execution. This results in a scorecard understood only at the top level, making it very difficult for those responsible for its results to understand the changes they have been faced with.

Senior management should be involved in the scorecard process, and should certainly show strong support for the initiative. They need to ensure that the scorecard is designed so that it applies to the entire organization, not just themselves. This way they will avoid the pitfall of the scorecard becoming a senior management project, while at the same time reinforce to employees their support and confidence in the initiative.

A Set of KPFs that Are Not Linked to Strategy

Just to review, one of the main purposes of the cascading process is to create KPFs that are linked to the overall organizational strategy. In other words, KPFs are supposed to be designed as a means to optimizing *global* organizational strategy and objectives, not local objectives. If an organization decides to take "shortcuts" in the scorecard process by determining a department's or an employee's KPFs without the cause-and-effect linkage created by a proper cascading process, there is a very high risk that the KPFs created will not reinforce the organization's strategy. If this is the case, employees may be motivated to take action that is not aligned with the organization's strategy — the main purpose of the scorecard initiative to begin with. It is therefore imperative that KPFs be linked to and aligned with strategy, and the only way to ensure that this is the case is through a proper cascade process.

Too Many Measures

A potential hazard in the construction of a scorecard system is assigning too many measures to determine performance results for a given goal. Too many measures are dangerous in two ways. First, there is a resulting increase in the amount of data collection and synthesis that must take place. Second, there is an increased risk of "information overload", which is when employees become overwhelmed with the amount of information they are expected to absorb. Either of these consequences is very undesirable, since they increase the unwanted likelihood of both employee resistance and confusion. Any given goal should not have more than two measures, except in rare circumstances. Overall the total number of measures should not outweigh the total number of goals by more than a factor of 1.5 to 1. Anything more can be hazardous to the success of the initiative.

In some recently conducted research, when companies were asked what pitfalls they had encountered, having too many measures was mentioned by ALL organizations. It therefore should be taken as a serious hazard, and steps consciously taken to avoid it from happening.

Scorecard Becomes "Just Another Report"

A key benefit of the scorecard is that it represents those few vital areas that merit the most attention from management and employees. Another way to look at it is, it really is a replacement of the other set of indicator reports that have been provided over the years. Designed properly, it will be a precise of the scores of reports employees have grown so accustomed to poring over every month (or quarter). With all this is mind, it is extremely important that the scorecard does not become just an additional report for management to spend time analyzing.

The negative effects of this approach are twofold. First, the meaning of the wealth of information provided in the scorecard will become diluted as it competes for attention with all the other reports. Second, human nature suggests that, given the choice, employees will stick with what they already know and understand. If the scorecard is not consciously and deliberately implemented as a replacement for other reports, it is doomed to become "just another report". Proper scorecard planning must incorporate the elimination (over time) of other reports, or at least making them less accessible. The scorecard should be the first source of information employees look to each month (or quarter). Designed properly, the scorecard will be the report that employees request anyway.

Scorecard that Has Not Incorporated Employee Participation

The importance of communication and solicitation of employee input has been discussed already. Still, it is one thing to request input, and quite another to actually incorporate it. It is extremely important to the success of the scorecard that employee input not just be sought, but be built into the scorecard system and promoted as such. Documentation should be kept tracking which employees have provided suggestions for the scorecard initiative, including which ideas have been included in the implementation. For ideas not factored in, a reason should be provided to the employee, with a note of appreciation and encouragement for coming forward with future suggestions. It is these types of steps that are usually considered unnecessary and overlooked, but may in the end dictate the success or failure of the implementation.

Summary

There are many factors that need to be considered when going forward with a scorecard initiative. Those discussed in this chapter merit special attention and all of them should be considered in the planning stage, as well as throughout the initiative.

Chapter 8

Looking Forward

Overview

> *"It is easy to perform a good action, but not easy to acquire a settled habit of performing such actions."*
>
> *—Aristotle*

Having made it this far into the balanced scorecard process, any organization is bound to reap the numerous benefits offered by scorecard implementation. The journey is not over, however. There are a variety of additional steps that should be considered to maintain and enhance the scorecard system. These steps will be the focus of this final chapter.

Rapid Prototyping

This book has exposed the reader to the fact that the balanced scorecard is no simple feat. While the approach proposed in the book makes the process much more straightforward, it cannot compensate for the fact that the balanced scorecard is a huge undertaking. This fact has made more than a few managers hesitant about embarking upon a scorecard initiative. For those in this particular situation, the next few paragraphs are good news indeed. A concept referred to as Rapid Prototyping can be the solution.

Created by Gary Cokins, an activity-based cost management expert, Rapid Prototyping is a method of rapidly creating and deploying an initiative in an off-line situation, so that the entire process can be experienced before going live. In this way, most, if not all, of the issues, challenges and questions that are inherent in an initiative can be faced and addressed before any real risks are taken. Cokins claims that Rapid Prototyping helps many organizations accomplish stellar results.

Does Rapid Prototyping translate well to the balanced scorecard? In a word: yes. A conversation with Cokins on this very topic confirms that Rapid Prototyping is useful not just in his arena, but lends itself well to the balanced scorecard. By rapidly creating a balanced scorecard and scoring it off-line in a non-threatening environment, an organization is able to confront many of the challenges inherent in employing a balanced scorecard. By encountering and fixing scorecard problems quietly and in a manner non-invasive to employees, the probability of success for a live scorecard implementation increases tremendously. In addition, the process is invaluable as a learning tool because it accelerates the learning process immensely and heightens familiarity with the scorecard process. This serves to drive out much of the natural fear and resistance that often accompany the balanced scorecard.

Rapid Prototyping can be considered a revolutionary way to introduce the organization to the balanced scorecard, since it allows organizations to make mistakes and correct them without allowing those mistakes to have any real impact. A good analogy is the castle versus the battlefield. In a war, a battlefield is no place to be trying new things, or testing new concepts. The consequences for those in battle (or employees in the field) can be far too severe. The place for that is in the castle, where ideas can be brought forward and considered without threat. Those in charge can then think through and test new ideas before bringing them to the battlefield. Rapid Prototyping is much like this because the ideas are brought forward and tested in a boardroom simulation. Then, the ideas that work are brought into the organization's mainline via a tested and proven scorecard.

There are several ways in which an organization can execute a Rapid Prototyping initiative. The most important element to consider is the initiative should quickly work through the entire balanced scorecard, from creation to scoring, at least twice. Also, it is important that a team of roughly four to six managers be established to execute the initiative, including at least one executive. It will require this amount of dedication to complete the initiative in a reasonable time.

Table 8-1 provides a snapshot of what a possible initiative might look like. The effort is best spread over a series of weeks (perhaps 10–12) to allow the scorecard to have actual month-end or quarter-end data entered into it so that actual results can be scored twice. Actual results can then be compared to expectations, lessons can be learned, and adjustments can be made as necessary. Initially, a time commitment of approximately one day per week will allow managers to make progress on the Rapid Prototyping initiative while still providing time for other duties. The Days of Effort column refers to number of days per team member. The entire initiative can be completed with a commitment of about six days per team member.

Like any initiative, the choice of whether to hire consultants will rest on many factors, such as organizational knowledge of the balanced scorecard, number of resources the organization is able to dedicate, and so on. Once the Rapid Prototyping initiative is complete, the organization should feel confident and comfortable enough to move forward with a complete implementation. Rapid Prototyping does not in any way provide a complete solution. Given the time frame involved and the level of commitment required, however, it can achieve impressive results and get an organization off to an excellent start.

Table 8-1

Possible Rapid Prototyping Initiative

Week	Days of Effort	Activity
1	1	Goals determination (I)
2	1	Goals determination (II)
3	1	Measures determination
4	1	Measures refinement; Target/stretch amount determination
2nd week after month-end	1	1st scoring process and follow-up
2nd week after next month-end	1	2nd scoring process and follow-up

Scorecard Process Improvement

Now that the scorecard initiative has been through an entire fiscal iteration, it is time to review the process and make changes based on what has been learned. For at least the first couple of fiscal scoring periods, the scorecard initiative should be considered a work in progress. It is important to continue seeking feedback and incorporating improvements into the process. This will assist in maximizing the likelihood of long-term success. There are many ways to collect feedback — an increasingly popular one is referred to as a "lessons learned" session, where key employees are brought together to share their insights on what they feel has gone well and not so well in the initial scorecard rollout. It is highly recommended that this, or some other formal mechanism of feedback collection be employed.

Another extremely important step is to take the feedback provided and make improvements based on it. The organization does not need to make every change suggested. Instead, a prioritization process should take place to determine which improvements provide the most "bang for the buck". The bottom line is, the scorecard implementation process does not conclude with the initial rollout. Like anything, there is a learning process involved and the opportunity for improvement should not be overlooked.

The Balanced Scorecard and Other Strategic Initiatives

To this point, the book has focused on the balanced scorecard in complete isolation from any other initiatives. The fact is, the scorecard can be an excellent tool to combine with other strategic initiatives. Since the scorecard is a framework tool that permeates the entire organization with respect to performance, it facilitates the merging of other tools within it as the organization strives toward achieving its strategy through performance management. While many strategic initiatives exist that could be performed in conjunction with the scorecard, two seem to have a particularly symbiotic relationship with the balanced scorecard: activity-based cost management and economic earnings.

The balanced scorecard does NOT need to be a stand-alone initiative. It is an excellent vehicle for integrating and communicating the many other initiatives that may be taking place concurrently with the scorecard. Some general examples of initiatives that could be incorporated into the balanced scorecard are:

- Quality and service management;

- Process-based thinking;

- Customer-relationship management; and

- Knowledge management.

The purpose of introducing concepts that can be merged with the balanced scorecard is not to raise questions without providing answers. Instead, the intent is to highlight the power of the balanced scorecard, and to demonstrate how very useful this tool can be when it comes to strategy fulfillment. Once a scorecard has been established, it may be useful to consider other strategic tools that can assist in achieving the goals stated in the scorecard. The intent of this section then is to give a strong indication of the synergies that can be realized by coupling the scorecard system with other tools.

vity-Based Cost Management

The balanced scorecard is an excellent tool for establishing clear targets aligned with strategy (in other words, it helps immensely with the "what" part of the strategy). One thing the scorecard does not provide in abundance is the "how" part of strategy that assists employees by providing the tools they need for strategy execution. One tool that has proven valuable in this capacity is referred to as activity-based cost management (ABCM). Also referred to as activity-based costing (ABC) or activity-based management (ABM), this tool can assist greatly with many of the objectives that are likely to appear on the organization's scorecard(s).

In his book on the topic, Gary Cokins[1] defines ABC as "…the mathematics used to reassign costs accurately to cost object, that is, outputs, products, services, customers. Its primary purpose is for profitability analysis." He goes on to say that ABCM "…uses ABC cost information to not only rationalize what products to sell but, more important, to identify opportunities to change the activities and processes to improve productivity."

vity-Based Cost Management and the Balanced Scorecard

Any organization implementing the balanced scorecard is likely going to need to arm itself with some other tools to assist it with the achievement of its chosen strategy. A tool like ABCM can prove extremely useful in this capacity.

nomic Profit

While the financial perspective has been downplayed in this book, the fact is that, in the long run, the financial perspective may just be the most important in terms of results, particularly for profit-seeking organizations. With this in mind, one of the questions often asked regarding the financial perspective is, "What types of goals and measures should be contained within this perspective?" An emerging trend in the world of finance and accounting is the use of the concept of economic profit as an evaluation of an organization's performance.

Economic profit is a concept that accounts for the cost of capital employed in the pursuit of profits, since there is an opportunity cost associated with the employment of capital. The normal approach to calculating economic profit is the traditional net income less a capital charge for assets employed. The capital charge is generally the actual capital employed multiplied by the organization's cost of capital:

Economic Profit=Net Income-(Capital * Cost of capital)

This approach is very logical since "true" financial performance should account for capital. For example, an organization that makes $1,000,000 in profits with $5,000,000 in capital has done better than another organization that makes $1,000,000 in profits with $10,000,000 in capital. To view it another way, if the first organization

---

[1] Gary Cokins, *Activity-Based Cost Management: Making It Work*, (New York: McGraw-Hill, 1996).

had an additional $5,000,000 in assets, they could have generated additional profits with them or, at bare minimum, let the funds sit in the bank earning interest. Five percent interest (roughly the risk-free interest rate) would yield an additional $250,000 in profits. So economic profit seems to be a much truer indicator of actual financial performance.

In addition to accounting for capital, economic profit can provide a truer picture of profits by making certain adjustments. For example, research and development is normally expensed as it is incurred, treatment made necessary by generally accepted accounted principles. Yet projects of this type are undertaken with one main purpose — to provide future value. This is consistent with the definition of an asset, not an expense. Economic profit recognizes this, and makes adjustments accordingly.

Other Strategic Initiatives: A Summary

Two tools, ABCM and economic profit, have been discussed briefly to give the reader a sense of the potential of the scorecard, beyond its capabilities as a stand-alone system. While these two tools should be given serious attention, the organization is by no means limited to consideration of these tools alone. Many other concepts may merit attention as well. The point to be made here is that the scorecard is not necessarily just a stand-alone item. Its flexibility allows for potential mingling with other initiatives, and this should be kept in mind during and after the scorecard initiative begins.

Final Thoughts

The balanced scorecard is a very logical and understandable approach to performance measurement and management. As time goes on it seems likely that a great deal of organizations will come to understand the benefits offered by the scorecard approach and decide to adopt it. There simply is no other tool available that can effectively align the entire workforce to the organizational strategy the way the scorecard can. While the decade following the emergence of the scorecard has not witnessed widespread proliferation of the tool, the numerous benefits of scorecard adoption suggest that its time will come. There is now ample evidence in business periodicals and presentations at seminars and conferences that the balanced scorecard is truly living up to the hype that surrounds it.

This book began with the assertion that the balanced scorecard is a powerful tool for performance measurement and management. It provides a solution to the age-old problem of how to align the actions of employees with the strategy of the organization, and how to reward employees for a "true" job well done. The word "true" is in quotes because in an ordinary organization, a job well done may or may not be associated with strategy fulfillment. Whether an employee's actions actually made a contribution toward the achievement of the organizational strategy may be impossible to determine, since objectives linked to strategy have never been established. In a balanced scorecard organization, however, employees do not need to "guess" if they are making a contribution toward the organizational strategy. The concept of employees having to face the "hit and miss" approach to job action is becoming an antiquated notion in the new millennium. The balanced scorecard should be the tool of choice for leaving it behind.

TOPICAL INDEX